We Are Heirs of the World's Revolutions

WE ARE HEIRS OF THE WORLD'S REVOLUTIONS

**Speeches from the Burkina Faso revolution
1983–87**

Thomas Sankara

Pathfinder

NEW YORK   LONDON   MONTREAL   SYDNEY

ISBN 978-0-87348-989-8
Library of Congress Control Number 2007936793
Manufactured in the United States of America

First edition, 2002
Second edition, 2007
Fifth printing, 2014

COVER DESIGN: Eric Simpson

COVER PHOTO: Damien Mabiala

FRONTISPIECE PHOTO: Thomas Sankara greets crowd in Orodara,
  Burkina Faso, 1986. (Margaret A. Novicki/Africa Report)

Pathfinder
www.pathfinderpress.com
E-mail: pathfinder@pathfinderpress.com

CONTENTS

THOMAS SANKARA

Thomas Sankara was the central leader of the popular, democratic revolution in the West African country of Burkina Faso (formerly Upper Volta) from 1983 to 1987.

Born in 1949, Sankara entered military school in 1966, one of the few avenues for young people of his generation to receive a higher education. Continuing his training in Madagascar in the early 1970s, he was strongly influenced by a massive uprising of workers and students that toppled the country's neocolonial government. It was in Madagascar that he was introduced to Marxism by students who had been part of the May 1968 prerevolutionary upsurge in France.

A lieutenant in Upper Volta's army, Sankara came to prominence as a military leader during a border conflict with Mali in December 1974 and January 1975. Over the next several years, he linked up with other junior officers and soldiers dissatisfied with the oppressive conditions in the country perpetuated by the imperialist rulers in Paris and elsewhere, with the support of local landlords, businessmen, tribal chieftains, and politicians.

Sankara was jailed briefly in 1982 after resigning a government post to protest the regime's repressive policies. In the wake of a coup, Sankara was appointed prime minister in January 1983. Sankara's uncompromising course—calling on the people of Upper Volta and elsewhere in Africa to advance their interests against the propertied exploiters at home and abroad—led to growing conflict with proimperialist forces in the government. In May 1983 Sankara and some of his supporters were arrested by President Jean-Baptiste Ouédraogo.

On August 4, 1983, some 250 soldiers marched from an insurgent military base in Pô to the capital of Ouagadougou. This act sparked a popular uprising, in which the Ouédraogo regime was overthrown. Sankara became president of the new National Council of the Revolution, opening four years of revolutionary activity by peasants, workers, women, and youth described in the pages that follow.

Sankara was assassinated and the revolutionary government was overthrown in a coup by Blaise Compaoré on October 15, 1987.

PREFACE

This preface is taken from remarks by Mary-Alice Waters, president of Pathfinder Press, to a February 10, 2005, presentation in Havana, Cuba, of the Spanish-language edition of *We Are Heirs of the World's Revolutions*. The event was organized as part of the annual Havana International Book Fair.

Also speaking on the panel were Manuel Agramonte, Cuba's ambassador to Burkina Faso during the four years of the revolutionary government led by Thomas Sankara; Armando Hart, one of the historic leaders of the Cuban Revolution and longtime minister of culture; and Ulises Estrada, director of *Tricontinental* magazine and himself an internationalist combatant with a long record of missions in Africa and Latin America.

∾

This booklet by Thomas Sankara, the leader of Burkina Faso's popular revolutionary government from 1983 to 1987, was published by Pathfinder Press in French and then English some three years ago. The publication of *Somos herederos de las revoluciones del mundo* means that now, for the first time ever, a few of Sankara's most important speeches are also available in Spanish. It is a powerful new weapon in the hands of those fighting to advance along the road first charted in the Communist Manifesto more than 150 years ago by Karl Marx and Frederick Engels and their comrades.

In October 1984, adopting a practice employed so effectively by Fidel [Castro] and Che [Guevara] before him, Thomas Sankara used the platform of the United Nations General Assembly to speak for and on behalf of the oppressed and exploited of the world. "I come here to bring you fraternal greetings from a country . . . whose seven million children, women, and men refuse to die from ignorance, hunger, and thirst any longer," Sankara told the assembled delegates of 159 nations.

"I make no claim to lay out any doctrines here. I am neither a messiah nor a prophet. I possess no truths. My only aspiration is . . . to speak on behalf of my people . . . to speak on behalf of 'the great disinherited people of the world,' those who belong to the world so ironically christened the Third World. And to state, though I may not succeed in making them understood, the reasons for our revolt."

Sankara voiced the determination and dignity of the people of one of the poorest countries of imperialist-ravaged Africa—one that then had the highest infant mortality rate in the world, a rural illiteracy rate approaching 98 percent, and an average life expectancy of some forty years. He reached out to, and spoke on behalf of, all those the world over who refuse to accept the economic bondage of class society and its consequences, including ecological devastation, social disintegration, racism, and the wars of conquest and plunder inevitably wrought by the workings of capitalism itself. Sankara knew such conditions are not "natural" phenomena, but the products of today's imperialist world order.

That world order, Sankara explained, can be fought, and must be destroyed. What marked him above all was his confidence in the revolutionary capacities of ordinary human beings to accomplish this. Like Fidel and Che, Sankara *believed* in the men and women so arrogantly dismissed by the rulers of the imperialist world. Sankara, as Fidel so memorably said of Che, did not think that man is "an incorrigible little animal, capable of advancing only if you feed him grass or tempt him with a carrot or whip him with a stick." Sankara, like Fidel, knew that anyone who thinks like that "will never be a revolutionary, . . . never be a socialist, . . . never be a communist."[1]

Sankara believed that a world built on different economic and social foundations can be created not by "technocrats," "financial wizards," or "politicians," but by the masses of workers and peasants whose labor, joined with the riches of nature, is the source of all wealth. By ordinary human beings who transform themselves as they become an active, conscious force, transforming their conditions of life. And the revolutionary government he headed set out along this course, mobilizing peasants, workers, craftsmen, women, youth, the elderly, to carry out a literacy campaign, an immunization drive, to sink wells, plant trees, build housing, and begin to eliminate the oppressive class relations on the land.

～

Sankara stood out among the leaders of the struggles for national liberation in Africa in the last half of the twentieth century because he was a communist. Unlike so many

---

1. Fidel Castro, October 8, 1987. Published as "Che's Ideas Are Absolutely Relevant Today," in Ernesto Che Guevara and Fidel Castro, *Socialism and Man in Cuba* (New York: Pathfinder, 1989).

others, he did not reject Marxism as a set of "European ideas," alien to the class struggle in Africa. He understood that Marxism is precisely *not* "a set of ideas," but the generalization of the lessons of the struggles of the working class on the road to its emancipation the world over, enriched by every battle. And he drew from those lessons to the best of his abilities.

Speaking before the United Nations in 1984, he linked the freedom struggle of the people of Burkina Faso to the centuries of revolutionary struggle from the birth of capitalism to today—from the American and French revolutions at the end of the eighteenth century to the great October Revolution of 1917 that "transformed the world, brought victory to the proletariat, shook the foundations of capitalism, and made possible the Paris Commune's dreams of justice." We are the heirs of those revolutions, he said—hence the title of this small book.

We are "open to all the winds of the will of the peoples of the world and their revolutions, having also learned from some of the terrible failures that led to tragic violations of human rights," he noted. "We wish to retain only the core of purity from each revolution. This prevents us from becoming subservient to the realities of others."

And along that line of march, Sankara looked to Cuba as the preeminent example of revolutionary struggle in our times.

~

Sankara was not only a leader of the people of Africa. He was not only a spokesman for the oppressed and exploited of the semicolonial countries. He gave leadership to working people in the imperialist world as well. In the last decades of the twentieth century, proletarian leaders with the world stature of Thomas Sankara, Maurice Bishop of Grenada, and in a similar way Malcolm X in the United States, have emerged from the ranks of the oppressed peoples of all lands—even the most economically undeveloped—to give leadership to the international struggle for national liberation and socialism. And thus to take their rightful place in history.

That fact is a measure of the vast changes that have marked the past century—the strengthening of revolutionary forces worldwide foreseen by [V.I.] Lenin and the leaders of the Communist International in the first years after the victory of the October Revolution.

This is the tradition in which we can today place the example given us by our five Cuban brothers who continue to fight not as victims, but as combatants of the Cuban Revolution placed by circumstances beyond their will on the front lines of the class struggle in the United States.[2] Within the federal prisons, where they are serving the draconian sentences the U.S. rulers imposed on them, they are carrying out their political work among some two million others who are the recipients of what Washington calls justice. That is where we see the original of the face

---

2. The Cuban Five—Fernando González, René González, Antonio Guerrero, Gerardo Hernández, and Ramón Labañino—were convicted in 2001 of charges including conspiracy "to act as an unregistered foreign agent," "to commit espionage," and "to commit murder." Sentences were handed down ranging from fifteen years, to terms of double life plus fifteen years. The five—each of whom has been named "Hero of the Republic of Cuba"—had accepted assignments to infiltrate counterrevolutionary groups in the United States and keep the Cuban government informed about terrorist attacks being planned against the Cuban people. Millions worldwide have mobilized to condemn the convictions, sentences, and harsh conditions of detainment and to demand their release.

that the whole world has witnessed so clearly at Guantánamo Bay Naval Base and in Iraq.[3]

∼

The books produced by Pathfinder are not sold only in
bookstores or through the worldwide web. Most are sold
on the streets—from sidewalk tables in working-class
districts of the cities and towns of the United States and
Europe, at mine portals and factory gates, on university
campuses and at high school doors, at demonstrations or
meetings where those who are fighting and seeking a way
forward for working people are likely to gather.

At those tables, the face of Thomas Sankara has a powerful, indeed unique impact. Many passing by are literally
stopped in their tracks when their eye falls on the book
Thomas Sankara Speaks—a substantial selection of his
speeches that Pathfinder published in English very soon
after he was assassinated in 1987. Some do not know who
Sankara is. But they are attracted to the confidence, character, and integrity they see in his face, and want to know
more about him.

It is among the growing tens of thousands of immi-
grant workers from West and Central Africa who today
are swelling the ranks of the working class in the imperialist centers, driven there by the whiplash of capital, that

---

3. Since early 2002, the U.S. government has used its Guantánamo naval
base in eastern Cuba—a piece of Cuba's territory held by Washington
against the will of the Cuban people—for a prison housing hundreds
seized primarily in Afghanistan as part of imperialism's "war on terror."
Deemed "enemy combatants," these prisoners have not been charged
with any crimes and have been subjected to brutality and torture, de-
nied contact with their families, and prevented from challenging their
detention in any court of law.

Sankara is best known and respected. Many are astonished to see the face of Sankara on a street table in the neighborhood where they live or work, on the cover of a book of his speeches, edited, printed, and distributed in the United States by working people there who look to Sankara as a revolutionary leader. That fact alone leads a good number to begin to think about the working class in the United States in a different way, and to be open to seeing the importance of the traditions of struggle they bring into what is the growing resistance by working people in North America to the bosses' assaults on our wages, job conditions, hours of work, and basic social and political rights.

And it is important to add that the converse is equally true. Reading Sankara is for us an important part of broadening the historical and cultural horizons of those who have been born or lived for years in the imperialist centers.

∼

Since it first appeared in 1988, close to 7,000 copies of *Thomas Sankara Speaks* have been sold in English alone, and many thousands more of the first French edition, *Oser inventer l'avenir*—dare to invent the future.

From the very beginning, one of the hallmarks of the revolutionary course Sankara fought for was the mobilization of women to fight for their emancipation. As he says in one of the speeches published here, an October 1983 talk that presents the program of the government he headed, "The revolution and women's liberation go together. We do not talk of women's emancipation as an act of charity or out of a surge of human compassion. It is a basic necessity for the revolution to triumph. Women hold up the other half of the sky."

Sankara's powerful speech to a gathering of several thousand women on International Women's Day, March 8, 1987—also contained in *Thomas Sankara Speaks*—has been published by Pathfinder as a pamphlet, *Women's Liberation and the African Freedom Struggle* that is available in four languages—French, English, Spanish, and Farsi. Some 12,000 copies of that title have been sold since it first appeared in English translation almost fifteen years ago—more than 1,500 in Farsi in Iran alone.

We are proud that with the publication of this selection of some of the most representative of Sankara's other speeches, his voice will now be heard more broadly in Spanish. *Somos herederos de las revoluciones del mundo* includes, for example, his powerful speech on imperialism's destruction of the trees and forests of Africa, given to an international conference in Paris in 1986.

Before top dignitaries of the French imperialist government, Sankara affirmed:

> The battle against the encroachment of the desert is a battle to establish a balance between man, nature, and society. As such, it is a political battle above all, and not an act of fate. . . .
>
> As Karl Marx said, those who live in a palace do not think about the same things, nor in the same way, as those who live in a hut. This struggle to defend the trees and forests is above all a struggle against imperialism. Imperialism is the arsonist setting fire to our forests and our savannahs.

That speech by Sankara is cited extensively in the recently produced issue number 13 of *New International* magazine, which is also being presented here today. From its lead article, entitled "Our Politics Start with the World," by Jack Barnes, to the photo of Earth at Night on its back cover—a photo that captures the economic and cultural inequalities, the veritable abyss, that exists between the imperialist and semicolonial countries, and among classes within almost every country—this issue of the magazine of Marxist politics and theory distributed by Pathfinder deals in depth with many of the same political issues and the course of action Sankara fought to advance.

~

To end, I want to point to the depth of Sankara's internationalism so evident in these pages. For him, the popular, democratic, revolutionary struggle of the people of Burkina Faso was one with the struggles to bring down the apartheid regime of South Africa; it was one with the anti-imperialist struggles of the people of Angola, Namibia, Palestine, Western Sahara, and Nicaragua; it was one with the people of Harlem who so warmly welcomed him there in 1984; it was one with the working people of France, the United States, and across the imperialist world.

It was in Managua in 1986 that I had the pleasure of meeting and coming to know Sankara as a leader. We were both delegates to an international conference marking the twenty-fifth anniversary of the founding of the Sandinista National Liberation Front (FSLN) and the tenth anniversary of the fall in combat of founding FSLN leader Carlos Fonseca. Sankara was chosen to speak at the rally on behalf of the 180 international delegations present there.

When he learned that a delegation from the Socialist Workers Party in the United States was present, he made a point of heading straight to our table to greet us. It was not just as an act of diplomacy; he came to talk politics with fellow revolutionists. He knew that the *Militant* newsweekly was one of the few papers outside Africa that regularly wrote about the revolutionary course unfolding in Burkina Faso, carrying interviews and speeches by Sankara whenever we could get them.

～

The presentation of *Somos herederos de las revoluciones del mundo* here in Cuba is especially appropriate because of the final selection it contains, Sankara's tribute to Che on October 8, 1987. That twentieth anniversary of Che's fall in combat was barely a week before the counterrevolutionary coup d'état that ended Sankara's own life.

It is only because of a fortunate combination of circumstances that Sankara's words at that memorable event are available to us today. The exhibition focusing on Che's revolutionary course and example, inaugurated that day by Sankara, coincided with the opening of an international antiapartheid conference in Ouagadougou attended by delegations from some twenty-nine countries. Among them were compañeros from the United States and Canada, supporters of the *Militant* newspaper, and of Pathfinder Press. They were looking at the displays when Sankara arrived together with Che's son Camilo and a number of other Cuban compañeros. When Sankara began his impromptu remarks, one of the Canadian compañeras pulled out a tape recorder she had in her backpack and recorded them. The *Militant* transcribed and published them shortly afterward, and they are included here in their totality.

Che taught us "we could dare to have confidence in ourselves and our abilities," Sankara pointed out on that occasion. Che instilled in us the conviction that "struggle is our only recourse."

Che, Sankara insisted, was "a citizen of the free world—
the free world that we're building together. That's why we
say that Che Guevara is also African and Burkinabè."
What more appropriate place to end?

Mary-Alice Waters

INTRODUCTION

On August 4, 1983, a popular uprising in the West African nation then known as Upper Volta initiated one of the most profound revolutions in Africa's history. A former colony of France, Upper Volta, with more than seven million inhabitants, was among the world's poorest countries.

The central leader of the revolution was Thomas Sankara, who became president of the new government at the age of thirty-three. A year later the people of Upper Volta adopted the name Burkina Faso—the Land of Upright Men.

Over a span of four years the popular revolutionary government organized the peasants, workers, and young people to carry out deep-going economic and social measures that curtailed the rights and prerogatives of the region's landed aristocratic and wealthy merchants. They joined with working people the world over to oppose imperialist domination. Mass organizations of peasants, craftsmen, workers, youth, women, and elders were initiated.

With broad popular support, the government abolished tribute payments and compulsory labor services to village chiefs. It nationalized the land to guarantee rural toilers—some 90 percent of the population—access to the fruits of their labors as productive farmers. The prices peasants received from the government for basic food crops were increased. The government launched tree-planting and irrigation projects to increase productivity and stop the advance of the Sahel desert region in the north of the country. It organized massive immunization campaigns, and made basic health care services available to millions. By 1985 infant mortality had fallen from 208 for every 1,000 live births at the beginning of the decade to 145, and the accelerated spread of parasite-induced river blindness had been curbed. In a country where illiteracy was 92 percent—and even higher in the countryside—literacy campaigns in its indigenous languages were initiated. Steps were taken to combat the age-old subjugation of women, who were encouraged to organize to fight for their emancipation. The government funded public works to build roads, schools, and housing. Trusting in the justice of the working class and peasantry, it set up popular revolutionary courts to try former leaders and high officials accused of corruption.

Led by Sankara, the Burkinabè Revolution charted a course of internationalist solidarity with those fighting oppression and exploitation in Africa and worldwide. Sankara championed the fight of the people of Western Sahara against the occupation of their country by Morocco and helped lead a successful fight to admit the Sahrawi representatives to the Organization of African Unity. He actively organized support, in Africa and beyond, for the struggle against the apartheid regime in South Africa and for the Palestinians' fight to reestablish their homeland. Sankara campaigned for cancellation of the onerous debt imposed on semicolonial countries by imperialist governments and banks. He spoke in New York City's Harlem to demonstrate support for African-Americans' fight against racist oppression and for other struggles by working people in the United States. He extended Burkina's hand to rising revolutionary struggles in Central America and the

Caribbean, visiting Cuba in 1984 and 1986, and Nicaragua in 1986, where he spoke on behalf of all the international guests at a 200,000-strong rally marking the twenty-fifth anniversary of the Sandinista National Liberation Front.

In August 1987, speaking in Burkina Faso on the anniversary of the revolutionary uprising four years earlier, Sankara emphasized that, "The democratic and popular revolution needs a convinced people, not a conquered people—a convinced people, not a submissive people passively enduring their fate." Growing numbers of workers, peasants, and youth issuing from the ranks of such a people were becoming involved in social and political life in Burkina Faso, setting an example that was already reverberating throughout Central West Africa—far beyond the borders of that landlocked country. But on October 15, 1987, Capt. Blaise Compaoré led a military coup serving the interests of those—at home and abroad—whose property and class domination were threatened by this deep-going revolutionary mobilization. Sankara and twelve of his aides and bodyguards were assassinated and the revolutionary government destroyed.

A week before his death, at a special commemoration in the capital of Ouagadougou, Sankara had spoken about Ernesto Che Guevara, the Argentine-born leader of the Cuban Revolution who died in combat twenty years earlier during an internationalist mission in Bolivia. In a speech reproduced in this book, Sankara, speaking of Che's legacy, noted that revolutionaries as individuals can be killed but "you cannot kill ideas." Thomas Sankara has himself become a symbol for millions of workers, peasants, and youth throughout Africa especially, who recognize in the Burkinabè Revolution—and in its continuing political heritage—a source of political ideas and inspiration for the battles for genuine liberation on the continent.

This book contains five speeches by Sankara:

- major excerpts of his October 1983 report to the Burkinabè people known as the "Political Orientation Speech" and broadcast on radio and television throughout the country;
- his October 1984 speech to the United Nations General Assembly in New York;
- his February 1986 presentation to an international conference in Paris on the preservation of trees;
- his February 1986 statement at the first summit meeting of the French-speaking world in Paris; and
- his October 1987 remarks at the opening in Ouagadougou of an exhibition on the life of Che Guevara.

These speeches offer a striking insight into the revolutionary political course explained and carried out in practice by Thomas Sankara to advance the interests of working people both inside and outside the country over the four years of the Burkinabè Revolution. More than two decades later, this proletarian internationalist perspective retains its relevance. The speeches published here remain a guide not only for hundreds of millions of peasants and workers of Africa and the rest of the semicolonial world where economic, social, and political conditions are worsening under the impact of the capitalist crisis. They constitute an essential component in the political arming of workers and farmers in the imperialist countries in North America, Europe, and Asia—working people who are confronted with the horrors the capitalist system of exploitation and oppression increasingly engenders at home as well as abroad.

∼

In the fall of 2007, on the twentieth anniversary of the overthrow of the revolutionary government in Burkina

Faso, Pathfinder published in English and French a new and expanded edition of *Thomas Sankara Speaks*. Originally published in 1988, just months after Sankara's murder, this collection of speeches and interviews remains the most complete record of one of the great revolutionary leaders of the modern working-class movement.

The present selection was initially published as a pamphlet in 2001. This new expanded edition includes a preface by Mary-Alice Waters, president of Pathfinder Press, based on her presentation to a meeting launching the Spanish edition, *Somos herederos de las revoluciones del mundo*, during the February 2005 Havana International Book Fair in Cuba. In addition to the new introduction and revised preface, the speeches appear here with larger, more readable type and an index.

Michel Prairie
July 2007

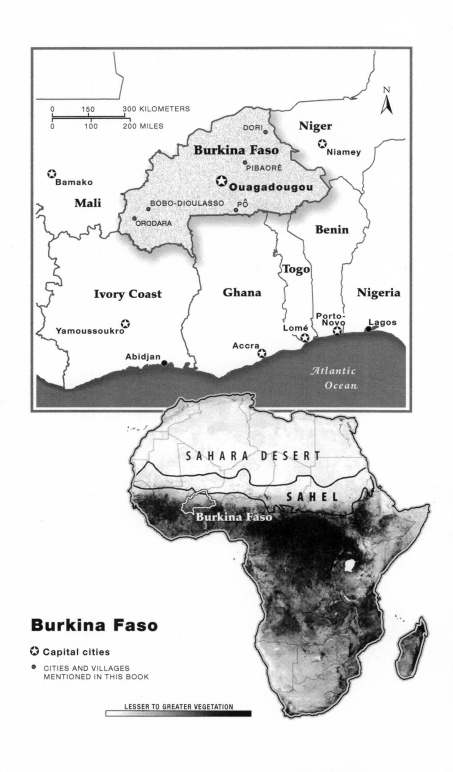

Burkina Faso

⊗ Capital cities

● CITIES AND VILLAGES
   MENTIONED IN THIS BOOK

LESSER TO GREATER VEGETATION

BURKINA FASO AT THE TIME OF THE REVOLUTION

POPULATION	7,964,705 (1985) (90% in rural areas)
NONAGRICULTURAL WORKERS	40,000 government 20,000 industrial (handicrafts & manufacturing) 10,000 construction
SURFACE AREA	105,869 sq. mi. / 274,200 sq. km
CAPITAL	Ouagadougou
AVERAGE YEARLY INCOME	US$150 (1981)

CURRENCY	CFA franc
	    During 1983–87, this fluctuated between 300 and
	    500 to the US dollar.

NATIONAL BUDGET	58 billion CFA francs (1985)
MAIN PRODUCTION & EXPORT GOODS	cotton, hides and skins, livestock, shea nut products, gold

ETHNIC GROUPS	Over 60, among them:
	    Mossi 53.0%
	    Peul 7.8%
	    Gourmantche 7.0%
	    Gurunsi 6.0%
	    Bissa 3.0%
	    Lobi 2.5%
	    Senufo 2.2%
	    Samo 2.0%
	    Marka 1.7%
	    Bobo 1.6%

LANGUAGES SPOKEN	Official language: French
	Over 60 spoken, among them:
	    Mooré 53.0%
	    Diula 8.8%
	    Fulfulde 6.6%

ILLITERACY	92% (98% in rural areas)
HEALTH	Life expectancy — 43.8 years (1980) Infant mortality rate — 208 per 1,000 live births (1981) Maternal mortality rate — 610 per 100,000 live births (1985) Doctors — 1 for every 37,494 (1988) Nurses — 1 for every 12,366 (1988) Midwives — 1 for every 28,397 (1988) Assistant midwives — 1 for every 31,267 (1988)

Upper Volta, mid-1970s. **Top**: Peasant irrigates field near Dori.
Bottom: Peasants plowing land.

Building a new society, rid of social injustice and imperialist domination

People of Upper Volta;

Comrade militants of the revolution:

In the course of this year, 1983, our country has gone through some particularly intense moments, whose impact still remains indelibly stamped on the minds of many of our fellow citizens. During this period, the struggle of the Voltaic people has experienced ebbs and flows.

Our people went through the test of heroic struggles and finally triumphed on the now historic night of August 4, 1983. The revolution has been irreversibly marching forward in our country now for almost two months. Two months during which the fighting people of Upper Volta have mobilized as one behind the National Council of the

---

Major excerpts from the "Political Orientation Speech," presented by Sankara on behalf of the National Council of the Revolution over Upper Volta radio and television. This speech became the revolution's major programmatic document.

Revolution in order to build a new, free, independent, and prosperous Voltaic society; a new society rid of social injustice and of the age-old domination and exploitation by international imperialism.

At the end of the short road traveled thus far, I invite you to take a look back with me, to draw the lessons necessary for accurately assessing the revolutionary tasks that are posed presently and for the near future. By equipping ourselves with a clear view of unfolding events, we strengthen ourselves all the more in our struggle against imperialism and reactionary social forces.

To sum up: Where have we come from? And where are we going? Those are the questions of the moment that demand a clear, resolute, and unequivocal answer from us, if we wish to march boldly forward to greater and more resounding victories.

The August revolution is the successful result of the Voltaic people's struggle

The triumph of the August revolution is due not only to the revolutionary takeover against the sacrosanct reactionary alliance of May 17, 1983.[1] It is the result of the Voltaic people's struggle against their long-standing enemies. It is a victory over international imperialism and its national allies. A victory over backward, obscurantist, and sinister forces. A victory over all the enemies of the people who have plotted and schemed behind their backs. . . .

The August revolution thus came as the solution to social contradictions that could no longer be suppressed by

---

1. On May 17, 1983, proimperialist forces in the government of Upper Volta staged a coup and arrested Prime Minister Thomas Sankara. Thousands took to the streets to demand his release, sparking resistance that was to culminate in the August 4 revolution.

compromise solutions.

The enthusiastic adherence of the broad popular masses to the August revolution is the concrete expression of the immense hopes that the Voltaic people place in the rise of the CNR. They hope that their deep-going aspirations might finally be achieved—aspirations for democracy, liberty, independence, genuine progress, and the restoration of the dignity and grandeur of our homeland, which twenty-three years of neocolonial rule have treated with singular contempt.

The legacy of twenty-three years of neocolonialism

The formation of the CNR on August 4, 1983, and the subsequent establishment of a revolutionary government in Upper Volta opened a glorious page in the annals of the history of our people and our country. However, the legacy bequeathed to us by twenty-three years of imperialist exploitation and domination is weighty and burdensome. Our task of building a new society cleansed of all the ills keeping our country in a state of poverty and economic and cultural backwardness will be hard and arduous.

In 1960 French colonialism—hounded on all sides, defeated at Dien Bien Phu, and grappling with tremendous difficulties in Algeria[2]—drew the lessons of those defeats and was compelled to grant our country its national sovereignty and territorial integrity. This was greeted positively by our people, who had not remained impassive, but rath-

---

2. Dien Bien Phu was the decisive final battle in Vietnam's war of national liberation against French colonialism. The surrender of the French forces there in May 1954 led to the end of French colonial presence in Indochina.

In November 1954 the National Liberation Front (FLN) of Algeria began a revolutionary war against French colonial occupation that led to the country's independence in 1962.

er had been developing appropriate struggles of resistance. This move by French colonial imperialism constituted a victory for the people over the forces of foreign oppression and exploitation. From the popular masses' point of view, it was a democratic reform, whereas from imperialism's point of view, it was merely a transformation of the forms of its domination and exploitation of our people.

This transformation nevertheless resulted in a realignment of classes and social layers and the formation of new classes. In alliance with the backward forces of traditional society, the petty-bourgeois intelligentsia of the time—with total contempt for the great masses, who they used as a springboard to power—set about laying the political and economic foundations for the new forms of imperialist domination and exploitation. Fear that the struggle of the popular masses might radicalize and lead to a genuinely revolutionary solution had been the basis for the choice made by imperialism: From that point on, it would maintain its stranglehold over our country and perpetuate the exploitation of our people through the use of Voltaic intermediaries. Voltaic nationals were to take over as agents of foreign domination and exploitation. The entire organization of neocolonial society would be nothing more than a simple operation of substituting one form for another.

In essence, neocolonial society and colonial society do not differ in the least. Thus, we saw the colonial administration replaced by a neocolonial administration identical to it in every respect. The colonial army was replaced by a neocolonial army with the same characteristics, the same functions, and the same role of safeguarding the interests of imperialism and its national allies. The colonial schools were replaced by neocolonial schools, which pursued the same goals of alienating the children of our country and reproducing a society fundamentally serving imperialist interests, and secondarily serving imperialism's local lackeys and allies.

With the support and blessing of imperialism, Voltaic nationals set about organizing the systematic plunder of our country. With the crumbs of this plunder that fell to them, they were transformed, little by little, into a genuinely parasitic bourgeoisie that no longer knew how to control its voracious appetite. Driven only by their own selfish interests, they no longer hesitated at employing the most dishonest means, engaging in massive corruption, embezzlement of public funds and properties, influence-peddling and real estate speculation, and practicing favoritism and nepotism.

This is what accounts for all the material and financial wealth they've been able to accumulate on the backs of working people. Not satisfied with living off the fabulous incomes they derive from shamelessly employing their ill-gotten wealth, they fight tooth and nail to monopolize political positions that will allow them to use the state apparatus for their own exploitative and wasteful ends.

Never do they let a year go by without treating themselves to extravagant vacations abroad. Their children desert the country's schools for prestigious educations in other countries. At the slightest illness, all the resources of the state are mobilized to provide them with expensive care at luxurious hospitals in foreign countries.

All this unfolds in full view of the honest, courageous, and hard-working Voltaic people, mired nonetheless in the most squalid misery. While Upper Volta is a paradise for the wealthy minority, for the majority—the people—it is a barely tolerable hell.

As part of this great majority, the wage earners, despite the fact that they are assured a regular income, suffer the constraints and pitfalls of capitalist consumer society. Their entire wage is spent before it has even been received. And this vicious cycle goes on and on with no perspective of being broken.

Within their respective trade unions, workers join in struggles around demands to improve their living conditions. The breadth of those struggles sometimes compels the neocolonial authorities to grant concessions. But they simply take back with one hand what they give with the other.

Thus a 10 percent wage increase is announced with great fanfare, only to be immediately taxed, wiping out the expected benefits. After five, six, or seven months, the workers always end up seeing through the swindle, and mobilize for new struggles. Seven months is more than enough for the reactionaries in power to catch their breath and devise new schemes. In this never-ending fight, the worker is always the loser.

Among this great majority are the peasants, the "wretched of the earth," who are expropriated, robbed, mistreated, imprisoned, scoffed at, and humiliated every day, and yet are among those whose labor creates wealth. Thanks to their productive labor, the country's economy stays afloat despite its frailty. It is from their labor that all those Voltaics for whom Upper Volta is an El Dorado line their pockets.

And yet, it is the peasants who suffer most from the lack of buildings, of road infrastructure, and from the lack of health care facilities and personnel. It is the peasants, creators of the nation's wealth, who suffer most from the lack of schools and school supplies for their children. It is their children who will swell the ranks of the unemployed after a brief stint on benches in schools that are poorly adapted to the realities of this country. It is among the peasants that the illiteracy rate is the highest—98 percent. Those who most need to learn, in order to improve the output of their productive labor, are again the ones who benefit the least from investments in health care, education, and technology.

The peasant youth—who have the same attitudes as all young people, that is, greater sensitivity to social injustice and a desire for progress—end up rebelling and they desert the countryside, thus depriving it of its most dynamic elements.

These youths' initial impulse drives them to the large urban centers, Ouagadougou and Bobo-Dioulasso. There they hope to find better-paying jobs and enjoy, too, the advantages of progress. The lack of jobs drives them to idleness, with all its characteristic vices. Finally, so as not to end up in prison, they seek salvation by going abroad, where the most shameless humiliation and exploitation await them. But does Voltaic society leave them any other choice?

Stated as succinctly as possible, such is the situation of our country after twenty-three years of neocolonialism—a paradise for some and hell for the rest.

After twenty-three years of imperialist domination and exploitation, our country remains a backward agricultural country, where the rural sector—employing 90 percent of the workforce—accounts for only 45 percent of the gross domestic product (GDP) and supplies 95 percent of the country's total exports.

More simply, it should be noted that in other countries, farmers constituting less than 5 percent of the population manage not only to feed themselves adequately and satisfy the basic needs of the entire nation, but also to export enormous quantities of their agricultural produce. Here, however, more than 90 percent of the population, despite strenuous exertions, experiences famine and deprivation and, along with the rest of the population, is compelled to fall back on imported agricultural products, if not on international aid.

The imbalance between exports and imports thus created accentuates the country's dependence on foreign countries. The resulting trade deficit has grown considerably over the years, and the value of our exports covers only around 25 percent of imports. To state it more clearly, we buy more from abroad than we sell abroad. And an economy that functions on such a basis increasingly goes bankrupt and is headed for catastrophe.

Private investments from abroad are not only insufficient, but also constitute a huge drain on the country's economy and thus do not help strengthen its ability to accumulate wealth. An important portion of the wealth created with the help of foreign investments is siphoned off abroad, instead of being reinvested to increase the country's productive capacity. In the 1973-79 period, it's estimated that 1.7 billion CFA francs left the country each year as income from direct foreign investments, while new investments came to only an average of 1.3 billion CFA francs a year.[3]

The insufficient level of productive investments has led the Voltaic state to play a fundamental role in the nation's economy through its efforts to compensate for the lack of

---

3. At 1983 exchange rates, these figures equaled approximately US$6.8 million leaving the country, compared with new investments of US$5.2 million.

Many of the former French colonies in Africa share a common currency, the CFA (African Financial Community) franc, whose convertibility with the French franc (and now the euro) is determined by Paris. At the time of the revolution, 1 French franc equaled 50 CFA francs. Based on the French franc's exchange rate, during 1983-87 the CFA franc fluctuated between 300 and 500 to the U.S. dollar.

private investment. This is a difficult situation, considering that the state's budgeted income basically consists of tax revenues, which represent 85 percent of total revenues and largely come from import duties and taxes.

In addition to making national investments, this income finances government spending, 70 percent of which goes to pay the salaries of civil servants and to ensure the functioning of administrative services. What, then, can possibly be left over for social and cultural investments?

In the field of education, our country is among the most backward, with 16.4 percent of children attending school and an illiteracy rate that reaches 92 percent on average. This means that of every 100 Voltaics, barely 8 know how to read and write in any language.

On the level of health, the rate of illness and mortality is among the highest in the subregion due to the proliferation of communicable diseases and nutritional deficiencies. How can such a catastrophic situation be avoided when we know that our country has only one hospital bed per 1,200 inhabitants and one doctor per 48,000 inhabitants?

These few elements alone suffice to illustrate the legacy left to us by twenty-three years of neocolonialism, twenty-three years of a policy of total national neglect. No Voltaic who loves and honors his country can remain indifferent to this most desperate situation.

Indeed our people, a courageous, hardworking people, have never been able to tolerate such a situation. Because they have understood that this was not an inevitable situation, but a question of society being organized on an unjust basis for the sole benefit of a minority. They have therefore waged different types of struggles, searching for the ways and means to put an end to the old order of things.

That is why they enthusiastically greeted the National Council of the Revolution and the August revolution.

These constitute the crowning achievement of the efforts they expended and the sacrifices they accepted so as to overthrow the old order, establish a new order capable of rehabilitating Voltaic man, and give our country a leading place within the community of free, prosperous, and respected nations.

The parasitic classes that had always profited from colonial and neocolonial Upper Volta are, and will continue to be, hostile to the transformations undertaken by the revolutionary process begun on August 4, 1983. The reason for this is that they are and remain attached to international imperialism by an umbilical cord. They are and remain fervent defenders of the privileges acquired through their allegiance to imperialism.

Regardless of what is done, regardless of what is said, they will remain true to themselves and will continue to plot and scheme in order to reconquer their "lost kingdom." Do not expect these nostalgic people to change their mentality and attitude. The only language they respond to and understand is the language of struggle, the revolutionary class struggle against the exploiters and oppressors of the people. For them, our revolution will be the most authoritarian thing that exists. It will be an act by which the people impose their will on them by all the means at their disposal, including arms, if necessary.

Who are these enemies of the people?

They revealed themselves in the eyes of the people during the May 17 events by their viciousness against the revolutionary forces. The people identified these enemies of the people in the heat of revolutionary action. They are:

1. The Voltaic bourgeoisie, which can be broken down, by the functions of its various layers, into the state bourgeoisie, the comprador bourgeoisie, and the middle bourgeoisie.

The state bourgeoisie. This is the layer known by the

label political-bureaucratic bourgeoisie. This is a bourgeoisie that has enriched itself in an illicit and criminal manner through its political monopoly. It has used the state apparatus just as an industrial capitalist uses his means of production to accumulate surplus value drawn from the exploitation of workers' labor power. This layer of the bourgeoisie will never willingly renounce its former privileges and sit by passively observing the revolutionary transformations under way.

The commercial bourgeoisie. This layer, by virtue of its business activity, is tied to imperialism through numerous bonds. For this layer, elimination of imperialist domination means the death of "the goose that lays the golden egg." That is why it will oppose the present revolution with all its might. Coming from this category, for example, are the corrupt merchants who seek to starve the people by taking food supplies off the market for purposes of speculation and economic sabotage.

The middle bourgeoisie. Although this layer of the Voltaic bourgeoisie has ties to imperialism, it competes with the latter for control of the market. But since it is economically weaker, imperialism supplants it. So it has grievances against imperialism. But it also fears the people, and this fear can lead it to make a bloc with imperialism. Nevertheless, since imperialist domination of our country prevents this layer from playing its real role as a national bourgeoisie, some of its members could, under certain circumstances, be favorable to the revolution, which would objectively place them in the people's camp. However, we must cultivate revolutionary mistrust between the people and individuals like these who come over to the revolution. Because all kinds of opportunists will rally to the revolution under this guise.

2. The reactionary forces that base their power on the

traditional, feudal-type structures of our society. In their majority, these forces were able to put up staunch resistance to French colonial imperialism. But ever since our country attained its national sovereignty, they have joined with the reactionary bourgeoisie in oppressing the Voltaic people. These forces have put the peasant masses in the position of being a reservoir of votes to be delivered to the highest bidder.

In order to safeguard their interests, which they share with imperialism in opposition to those of the people, these reactionary forces most frequently rely on the decaying and declining values of our traditional culture that still endure in rural areas. To the extent that our revolution aims to democratize social relations in the countryside, giving more responsibilities to the peasants, and making more education and knowledge available to them for their own economic and cultural emancipation, these backward forces will oppose it.

These are the enemies of the people in the present revolution, enemies that the people themselves identified during the May events. These are the individuals who made up the bulk of the isolated marchers who, protected by a cordon of soldiers, demonstrated their class support for the already moribund regime that had emerged from the reactionary and proimperialist coup.

The rest of the population, aside from the reactionary and antirevolutionary classes and social layers enumerated above, is what comprises the Voltaic people. A people who consider imperialist domination and exploitation to be an abomination and who have continually demonstrated this by concrete, daily struggle against the various neocolonial regimes. In the present revolution the people consist of:

1. The Voltaic working class, young and few in number, but which, through unremitting struggle against the

bosses, has been able to prove that it is a genuinely revolutionary class. In the present revolution, it is a class that has everything to gain and nothing to lose. It has no means of production to lose, it has no piece of property to defend within the framework of the old neocolonial society. It is convinced, however, that the revolution is its business, because it will emerge from it in a stronger position.

2. The petty bourgeoisie, which constitutes a vast, very unstable social layer, that quite often vacillates between the cause of the popular masses and that of imperialism. In its large majority, it always ends up by taking the side of the popular masses. It includes the most diverse components, including small shopkeepers, petty-bourgeois intellectuals (civil servants, college and high school students, private sector employees, etc.), and artisans.

3. The Voltaic peasantry, which in its big majority consists of small peasants, who are tied to small plots of land because of the gradual disintegration of collective property forms since the introduction of the capitalist mode of production in our country. Market relations have increasingly dissolved communal bonds and replaced them with private property over the means of production. In the new situation thus created by the penetration of capitalism into our countryside, the Voltaic peasant, tied to small-scale production, embodies bourgeois productive relations. Given all these considerations, the Voltaic peasantry is an integral part of the category of the petty bourgeoisie.

Because of the past and its present situation, the peasantry is the social layer that has paid the highest toll for imperialist domination and exploitation. The economic and cultural backwardness that characterizes our countryside has long kept the peasantry isolated from the great currents of progress and modernization, relegating it to the role of reservoir for reactionary political parties. Nevertheless, the peasantry has a stake in the revolution and, in terms of numbers, is its principal force.

4. The lumpenproletariat. This is the category of declassed individuals who, since they are without jobs, are prone to hire themselves out to reactionary and counter-revolutionary forces to carry out the latter's dirty work. To the extent that the revolution can provide them something useful to do, they can become its fervent defenders.

The character and scope of the August revolution

The revolutions that occur around the world are not at all alike. Each revolution presents original features that distinguish it from the others. Our revolution, the August revolution, is no exception. It takes into account the special features of our country, its level of development, and its subjugation by the world imperialist capitalist system.

Our revolution is a revolution that is unfolding in a backward, agricultural country, where the weight of tradition and ideology emanating from a feudal-type social organization weighs very heavily on the popular masses. It is a revolution in a country that, because of imperialism's domination and exploitation of our people, has evolved from a colony into a neocolony.

It is a revolution occurring in a country still characterized by the lack of an organized working class conscious of its historic mission, and which therefore possesses no tradition of revolutionary struggle. It is a revolution occurring in a small country on the continent, at a time when, on the international level, the revolutionary movement is coming apart day by day, without any visible hope of seeing a homogenous bloc arise capable of giving a stimulus and practical support to nascent revolutionary movements. This set of historical, geographic, and sociological circumstances gives a certain, specific stamp to our revolution.

The August revolution exhibits a dual character: It is a democratic and a popular revolution.

Its primary tasks are to eliminate imperialist domination and exploitation; and to purge the countryside of all the social, economic, and cultural obstacles that keep it in a backward state. Its democratic character flows from this. It draws its popular character from the full participation of the Voltaic masses in the revolution, and their consistent mobilization around democratic and revolutionary slogans that concretely express their own interests in opposition to those of the reactionary classes allied with imperialism. The popular character of the August revolution also lies in the fact that, in place of the old state machinery, new machinery is being built, capable of guaranteeing the democratic exercise of power by the people and for the people.

Our present revolution as characterized above, while being an anti-imperialist revolution, is still unfolding within the framework of the limits of the bourgeois economic and social order. By analyzing the social classes of Voltaic society, we have put forward the idea that the Voltaic bourgeoisie does not constitute a single, homogenous, reactionary, and antirevolutionary mass. Indeed, what characterizes the bourgeoisie in underdeveloped countries under capitalist relations is its congenital inability to revolutionize society as the bourgeoisie of the European countries did in the 1780s, that is, at the time when it still constituted a rising class.

Such are the characteristics and limitations of the present revolution launched in Upper Volta on August 4, 1983. Having a clear view and precise definition of its content guards us against the dangers of deviation and excesses that could be detrimental to the victorious march of the revolution. All those who have taken up the cause of the

August revolution should fix firmly in their minds the guiding principles laid out here. By doing so they can assume their role as conscious revolutionaries. And, as genuine, bold, and tireless propagandists, they can disseminate these principles among the masses.

It is no longer enough to call oneself a revolutionary. We also need to be absolutely clear on the profound meaning of the revolution we fervently defend. This is the best way to defend it from the attacks and distortions that the counter-revolutionaries will not fail to use against it. Knowing how to link revolutionary theory to revolutionary practice will be the decisive criterion from now on in distinguishing consistent revolutionaries from all those who flock to the revolution under motives that are alien to the revolutionary cause.

On popular sovereignty in the exercise of revolutionary power

As we have said, one of the distinctive traits of the August revolution and which endows it with its popular character, is that it is a movement of the vast majority for the benefit of the vast majority.

It is a revolution made by the Voltaic popular masses themselves, with their own slogans and aspirations. The goal of this revolution consists in having the people assume power. That is the reason why the first act of the revolution, following the August 4 proclamation, was the appeal addressed to the people to create Committees for the Defense of the Revolution [CDRs].[4] The National Council

---

4. The Committees for the Defense of the Revolution (CDRs) were mass organizations developed after the revolutionary victory, based in neighborhoods, villages, workplaces, schools, and army units throughout the country. The CDRs mobilized participation in social programs of the revolutionary government, drawing the population into political activity.

of the Revolution is convinced that for this revolution to be a genuinely popular revolution, it must proceed to destroy the neocolonial state machinery and organize new machinery capable of guaranteeing popular sovereignty. The question of knowing how this popular power will be exercised, how this power should be organized, is an essential question for the future of our revolution.

Until today, the history of our country has essentially been dominated by the exploiting and conservative classes, which have exercised their antidemocratic and antipopular dictatorship through their stranglehold on politics, the economy, ideology, culture, the administration, and the judicial system.

The primary goal of the revolution is to transfer power from the hands of the Voltaic bourgeoisie allied with imperialism to the hands of the alliance of popular classes that constitute the people. This means that from now on the people, who hold power, will have to counterpose their democratic and popular power to the antidemocratic, antipopular dictatorship of the reactionary alliance of social classes that favor imperialism.

This democratic and popular power will be the foundation, the solid basis, of revolutionary power in Upper Volta. Its chief task will be the total conversion of the entire state machinery with its laws, administration, courts, police, and army, which have been fashioned to serve and defend the selfish interests of the reactionary social classes and layers. Its task will be to organize the struggle against the counterrevolutionary intrigues seeking to reconquer "Paradise Lost," on the road to completely crushing the resistance of the reactionaries who are nostalgic for the past. Therein lies the need for and the role of the CDRs as the base of operations for the popular masses as they storm the citadels of reaction and counterrevolution. . . .

For revolutionizing all sectors of Voltaic society

All the previous political regimes, one after the other, until now have strived to introduce measures to better run neocolonial society. The changes introduced by these regimes amounted to installing new teams within the continuity of neocolonial power. None of these regimes wished nor was able to question the socioeconomic foundations of Voltaic society. That is why they all failed.

The August revolution does not aim to establish one more regime in Upper Volta. It represents a break with all previously known regimes. Its ultimate goal is to build a new Voltaic society, within which the Voltaic citizen, driven by revolutionary consciousness, will be the architect of his own happiness, a happiness equal to the efforts he will have made.

To do this, the revolution—whether the conservative and backward forces like it or not—will be a deep and total upheaval that will spare no domain, no sector of economic, social, and cultural activity.

Revolutionizing all domains and all sectors of activity is the slogan of the day. Strengthened by the guiding principles laid out here, each citizen should work to revolutionize his sector of activity, wherever he finds himself.

The philosophy of revolutionary transformations is already affecting the following sectors: (1) the national army; (2) policies concerning women; and (3) economic development.

(1) The national army: its place in the democratic
and popular revolution

According to the defense doctrine of revolutionary Upper Volta, a conscious people cannot leave their homeland's defense to one group of men, however competent they may be. Conscious people take charge themselves of their homeland's defense. To this end, our armed forces constitute simply a detachment that is more specialized than the rest of the population for Upper Volta's internal and external security requirements. Similarly, even though the health of the Voltaic people is the business of the people and of each individual Voltaic, there exists and will continue to exist a more specialized medical corps that devotes more time to the question of public health.

The revolution imposes three missions on the national armed forces:

1. To be capable of combating all internal and external enemies and to participate in the military training of the rest of the people. This presupposes an increased operational capacity, making each soldier a competent fighter, unlike the old army, which was merely a mass of employees.

2. To participate in national production. Indeed, the new soldier must live and suffer among the people to which he belongs. The days of the free-spending army are over. From now on, besides handling arms, the army will work in the fields and raise cattle, sheep, and poultry. It will build schools and health clinics and ensure their functioning. It will maintain roads and will transport mail, the sick, and agricultural products between regions by air.

3. To train each soldier as a revolutionary militant. Gone are the days when the army was declared to be neutral and apolitical, while in fact serving as the bastion of reaction and the guardian of imperialist interests. Gone are the days when our national army conducted itself like a corps of foreign mercenaries in conquered territory. Those days are gone forever. Armed with political and ideological training, our soldiers, noncommissioned officers, and officers engaged in the revolutionary process will no longer be potential criminals, but will instead become conscious revolutionaries, at home among the people like a fish in water.

As an army at the service of the revolution, the National Popular Army will have no place for any soldier who looks down on, scorns, or brutalizes his people. An army of the people at the service of the people—such is the new army we are building in place of the neocolonial army, which was utilized to rule over the people as a veritable instrument of oppression and repression in the hands of the reactionary bourgeoisie. Such an army, even in terms of its internal organization and its principles of functioning, will be fundamentally different from the old army. Thus, instead of blind obedience of soldiers toward their officers, of subordinates toward their superiors, a healthy discipline will be developed that, while strict, will be based on its conscious acceptance by the men and the troops.

Contrary to the opinions of reactionary officers fostered by a colonial attitude, the politicization of the army, its revolutionization, does not signal the end of discipline. Discipline in a politicized army will have a new content. It will be a revolutionary discipline. That is, a discipline that derives its strength from the fact that the human dignity of the officer and the soldier, of the commissioned and noncommissioned personnel, is worth the same, and that they differ from one another only with regard to their concrete tasks and respective responsibilities. Armed with this understanding of the relations between men, military cadres must respect their men, love them, and treat them as equals.

Here too the Committees for the Defense of the Revolution have a fundamental role to play. CDR militants within the army must be tireless pioneers in building the National Popular Army of the democratic and popular state, whose essential tasks internally will be to defend the rights and interests of the people, maintain revolutionary order, and safeguard democratic and popular power; its task externally will be to defend our territorial integrity.

*(2) The Voltaic woman: her role in the democratic
and popular revolution*

The weight of age-old traditions in our society has relegated women to the rank of beasts of burden. Women suffer doubly from all the scourges of neocolonial society. First, they experience the same suffering as men. Second, they are subjected to additional suffering by men.

Our revolution is in the interests of all the oppressed and all those who are exploited in today's society. It is therefore in the interests of women, since the basis of their domination by men lies in the system through which society's political and economic life is organized. By changing the social order that oppresses women, the revolution creates the conditions for their genuine emancipation.

The women and men of our society are all victims of imperialist oppression and domination. That is why they wage the same battle. The revolution and women's liberation go together. We do not talk of women's emancipation as an act of charity or out of a surge of human compassion. It is a basic necessity for the revolution to triumph. Women hold up the other half of the sky.

Forging a new mentality among Voltaic women that allows them to take responsibility for the country's destiny alongside men is one of the essential tasks of the revolution. The same is true of the transformation to be made in men's attitudes toward women.

Until now, women have been excluded from the realm of decision making. The revolution, by entrusting women with responsibilities, is creating the conditions for unleashing women's fighting initiative. As part of its revolutionary policy, the CNR will work to mobilize, organize, and unite all the dynamic forces of the nation, and women will not be left behind. They will be involved in all the battles we will have to wage against the various shackles of neocolonial society in order to build a new society. They will be involved at all levels in conceiving projects, making decisions, and implementing them—in organizing the life of the nation as a whole. The final goal of this great undertaking is to build a free and prosperous society in which women will be equal to men in all spheres.

However, we must have a correct understanding of the question of women's emancipation. It is not a mechanical equality between men and women, acquiring habits recognized as male—drinking, smoking, and wearing pants. That's not the emancipation of women. Nor will acquiring diplomas make women equal to men or more emancipated. A diploma is not a free pass to emancipation.

The genuine emancipation of women is one that entrusts responsibilities to women, that involves them in productive activity and in the different fights the people face. The genuine emancipation of women is one that compels men to give their respect and consideration. Emancipation, like freedom, is not granted, it is conquered. It is for women themselves to put forward their demands and mobilize to win them.

For that, the democratic and popular revolution will create the necessary conditions to allow Voltaic women to achieve total and complete fulfillment. For could it be possible to eliminate the system of exploitation while maintaining the exploitation of women, who make up more than half our society?

(3) The national economy: independent, self-sufficient, and planned at the service of a democratic and popular society

The process of revolutionary transformations undertaken since August 4 places major democratic and popular reforms on the agenda. The National Council of the Revolution is therefore aware that the construction of an independent, self-sufficient, and planned national economy requires the radical transformation of present society, a transformation that itself requires the following major reforms:

- Agrarian reform.
- Administrative reform.
- Educational reform.
- Reform of the structures of production and distribution in the modern sector.

The agrarian reform will aim to:

- Increase labor productivity through better organization of the peasants and the introduction of modern agricultural techniques in the countryside.
- Develop a diversified agriculture, together with regional specialization.
- Abolish all the fetters that are part of the traditional socioeconomic structures that oppress the peasants.
- Finally, make agriculture the basis for the development of industry.

All this is possible by giving real meaning to the slogan of food self-sufficiency, a slogan that now seems dated for having been proclaimed so often without conviction. First, this will be a bitter struggle against nature, which, by the way, is no more thankless for us than for other peoples who have conquered it magnificently on the agricultural level. The CNR will harbor no illusions in gigantic, sophisticated projects. To the contrary, numerous small accomplishments in the agricultural system will allow us to transform our territory into one vast field, an endless series of farms.

Second, this will be a struggle against those who starve the people, the agricultural speculators and capitalists of all types. Finally, it will mean protecting our agriculture against domination by imperialism—with regard to its orientation, the plunder of our resources, and unfair competition from imports against our local products, imports whose only advantage is their packaging aimed at bourgeois afflicted with snobbishness. As for the peasants, sufficiently high prices and industrial food-processing facilities will guarantee them markets for their produce in any season.

The administrative reform aims to make operational the administration inherited from colonialism. To do that, it must be rid of all the evils that characterize it—namely, the unwieldy and nitpicking bureaucracy and its consequences—and a complete revamping of the civil service statutes must be undertaken. The reform should result in a less costly, more effective, and more flexible administration.

The educational reform aims to promote a new orientation for education and culture. It should result in transforming the schools into instruments at the service of the revolution. Graduates of the system should not serve their own interests and the exploiting classes, but rather the popular masses. The revolutionary education that will be taught in the new schools must imbue everyone with a Voltaic ideology, a Voltaic personality that rids the individual of blind mimicry. One of the jobs of education in a democratic and popular society will be to teach students to assimilate the ideas and experiences of other peoples in a critical and positive manner.

To end illiteracy and obscurantism, emphasis will have to be placed on mobilizing all energies, with the idea of organizing the masses, to increase their awareness and induce in them a thirst for knowledge by showing them the drawbacks of ignorance. Any policy of fighting illiteracy without the participation of those most concerned is doomed to failure.

Culture in a democratic and popular society, should have a three-fold character: national, revolutionary, and popular. Everything that is antinational, antirevolutionary, and antipopular must be banished. To the contrary, our culture extols dignity, courage, nationalism, and the great human virtues.

The democratic and popular revolution will create favorable conditions for the blossoming of a new culture. Our artists will have a free hand to go boldly forward. They should seize the opportunity before them to raise our culture to a world level. Let writers put their pens at the service of the revolution. Let musicians sing not only of our people's glorious past, but also of their radiant and promising future.

The revolution expects our artists to be able to describe reality, portray it in living images, and express them in melodious tunes while showing our people the true way forward to a better future. It expects them to place their creative genius at the service of a national, revolutionary, and popular Voltaic culture.

We must be able to draw on what is positive from the past—that is, from our traditions, and what is positive in foreign cultures—in order to give a new dimension to our culture. The inexhaustible source for the masses' creative inspiration lies within the popular masses. Knowing how to live with the masses, becoming involved in the popular movement, sharing the joys and sufferings of the people, and working and struggling with them—all these should be the major concerns of our artists. Before producing, they should ask themselves: for whom is our creation intended? If we are convinced that we are creating for the people, then we must understand clearly who the people are, what their different components are, and what their deepest aspirations are.

The reform of our economy's structures of production and distribution seek to increasingly establish effective control by the Voltaic people over the channels of production and distribution. For without genuine control over these channels, it is practically impossible to build an independent economy at the service of the people.

People of Upper Volta;

Comrade militants of the revolution:

The needs of our people are immense. Satisfaction of these needs requires that revolutionary transformations be undertaken in all fields.

In the field of health care and social assistance for the popular masses, the goals to be achieved can be summed up as follows:

• Making health care available to everyone.

• Setting up maternal and infant assistance and care.

• A policy of immunization against communicable diseases by increasing the number of vaccination campaigns.

• Raising the masses' awareness of the need to acquire good habits of hygiene.

All these goals can be attained only with the conscious involvement of the popular masses themselves in this fight, under the revolutionary guidance of the health services.

In the field of housing—a field of crucial importance—we must undertake a vigorous policy to end real estate speculation and the exploitation of workers through rent-gouging. Important measures in this field must be taken:

• Setting reasonable rents.

• Rapidly dividing neighborhoods into lots.

• Undertaking large-scale construction of modern residential homes, in sufficient numbers and accessible for workers.

One of the CNR's essential concerns is to unite the different nationalities that exist in Upper Volta in the common struggle against our revolution's enemies. There are indeed in our country a multitude of ethnic groups that differ from each other in language and customs. The Voltaic nation consists of the totality of these nationalities. Imperialism, through its policy of divide and rule, strove to exacerbate the contradictions among them, to set one against the other.

The CNR's policy aims to unite these different nationalities so that they live on an equal basis and enjoy equal opportunities for success. To do that, special emphasis will be placed on:

- Promoting economic development of the different regions.
- Encouraging economic exchanges between them.
- Combating prejudices between the ethnic groups, resolving in a spirit of unity the differences that divide them.
- Punishing those who foment divisions.

In view of all the problems that our country faces, the revolution can be described as a challenge that we must rise to. We do so driven by the will to victory, and together with the active participation of the popular masses mobilized through the CDRs.

In the near future, with the elaboration of programs for the various sectors, the entire territory of Upper Volta will be one vast construction site. The participation of all Voltaics able and old enough to work will be needed in the ruthless fight we will be waging to transform this country into a prosperous and radiant country, a country where the people will be the only masters of the nation's material and spiritual wealth.

Finally, we must define the place of the Voltaic revolution in the world revolutionary process. Our revolution is an integral part of the world movement for peace and democracy, against imperialism and all forms of hegemonism. That is why we will strive to establish diplomatic relations with other countries, regardless of their political and economic systems, on the basis of the following principles:

- Respect for each other's independence, territorial integrity, and national sovereignty.
- Mutual nonaggression.
- Noninterference in domestic affairs.
- Trade with all countries on an equal footing and on the basis of mutual benefit.

We will give active solidarity and support to national liberation movements fighting for the independence of their countries and the liberation of their peoples. This support is directed in particular:

- To the Namibian people, under the leadership of SWAPO.
- To the Saharawi people, in their struggle to recover their national territory.
- To the Palestinian people, for their national rights.

Objectively, the anti-imperialist African countries are allies in our struggle. The neocolonial alliances operating on our continent make closer ties with these countries necessary.

Long live the democratic and popular revolution!
Long live the National Council of the Revolution!
Homeland or death, we will win!

Top: Second anniversary of the Burkinabè Revolution, August 1985.
Bottom: Peasants' rally, Pibaoré, October 1987. Banner reads: "Farmers of Burkina Faso: hoes yesterday, hoes today, machinery tomorrow."

Top: Sankara addresses the UN General Assembly, October 1984. **Bottom**: Cuban President Fidel Castro welcomes Sankara to Havana, September 1984.

Freedom must be conquered in struggle

Mr. President;

Mr. Secretary General;

Honorable representatives of the international community:

I come here to bring you fraternal greetings from a country of 274,000 square kilometers whose seven million children, women, and men refuse to die of ignorance, hunger, and thirst any longer. In their quarter century of existence as a sovereign state seated at the UN, they have been unable to really live.

I come to address you at this Thirty-ninth Session on behalf of a people who, in the land of their ancestors, have decided to henceforth assert themselves and accept their history—both its positive and negative aspects—without the slightest complex.

Sankara delivered this address to the Thirty-ninth Session of the United Nations General Assembly in New York. His speech was published as a pamphlet by the Permanent Mission of Burkina Faso to the United Nations.

I come here, finally, mandated by the National Council of the Revolution of Burkina Faso, to express the views of my people concerning the problems on the agenda—consisting of the tragic web of events that are painfully cracking the foundations of our world at the end of the twentieth century. A world in which humanity has been transformed into a circus, torn apart by struggles between the great and the semi-great, attacked by armed bands, and subjected to violence and pillage. A world in which nations, eluding international law, command groups of outlaws who, guns in hand, live by plunder and organize sordid trafficking.

Mr. President:

I make no claim to lay out any doctrines here. I am neither a messiah nor a prophet. I possess no truths. My only aspiration is twofold: first, to be able to speak on behalf of my people, the people of Burkina Faso, in simple words, words that are clear and factual. And second, in my own way to also speak on behalf of the "great disinherited people of the world," those who belong to the world so ironically christened the Third World. And to state, though I may not succeed in making them understood, the reasons for our revolt.

All this indicates our interest in the United Nations. We understand that demanding our rights requires from us a vigorous and rigorous awareness of our duties.

No one will be surprised to see us associate the former Upper Volta, today Burkina Faso, with that hodgepodge held in such contempt—the Third World—invented by the other worlds as many countries became formally independent in order to better ensure our intellectual, cultural, economic, and political alienation.

We want to place ourselves within this world, without lending any credence to that gigantic fraud of history, and certainly without accepting the status of "hinterland of a satiated West." Rather, we want to assert our awareness of belonging to a tricontinental whole and, with the force of deeply felt convictions, acknowledge, as a Nonaligned country, that there is a special relationship of solidarity uniting the three continents of Asia, Latin America, and Africa in a single struggle against the same political traffickers, the same economic exploiters.

Therefore, recognizing that we are part of the Third World means, to paraphrase José Martí, "asserting that our cheek feels the blow struck against any man in the world." Up to now we have turned the other cheek. The blows increased. But the wicked-hearted were not moved. They trampled the truth of the righteous. The word of Christ was betrayed. His cross was transformed into a club. And after they put on his robe, they slashed our bodies and souls. They obscured his message. They Westernized it, whereas we had understood it as one of universal liberation. Then our eyes opened to the class struggle. There will be no more blows.

It must be proclaimed that there can be no salvation for our peoples unless we decisively turn our backs on all the models that all the charlatans, cut from the same cloth, have tried to sell us for the past twenty years. There can be no salvation without saying no to that. No development without breaking with that.

Moreover, all the new "intellectual leaders" emerging from their slumber, awakened by the dizzying rise of billions of men in rags, aghast at the threat that this famished multitude presents to their digestion, are beginning to revamp their speeches. In an anxious quest, they are looking in our direction once again, for miracle concepts and new forms of development for our countries. It's enough to read the numerous proceedings of innumerable symposiums and seminars to be convinced of this.

Far be it from me to ridicule the patient efforts of those honest intellectuals who, because they have eyes to see, are discovering the terrible consequences of the devastation imposed by the so-called specialists in Third World development. The fear haunting me is that the fruit of so much effort may be commandeered by Prosperos of all kinds to make a magic wand, designed to return us to a world of slavery redone in the fashion of the day.[1]

This fear is even more justified by the fact that the educated petty bourgeoisie of Africa—if not the Third World— is not prepared to give up its privileges, either due to intellectual laziness or simply because it has tasted the Western way of life. So it forgets that any genuine political struggle requires rigorous, theoretical debate, and it refuses to make the effort to think out and invent new concepts equal to the murderous fight awaiting us. A passive and pathetic consumer, the petty bourgeoisie abounds in terminology fetishized by the West, just as it abounds in Western whiskey and champagne, enjoyed in lounges of dubious taste.

We would search in vain for genuinely new ideas that have emanated from the minds of our "great" intellectuals since the emergence of the now-dated concepts of Negritude and African Personality.[2] The vocabulary and ideas

---

1. In William Shakespeare's play *The Tempest*, Prospero is a sorcerer who uses his power to control the fate of others. In the eyes of many anticolonial fighters in the twentieth century, Prospero came to symbolize the oppressors.

2. Negritude was a literary movement that began among French-speaking African and Caribbean writers living in Paris in the 1930s. Formed as a protest against French rule and its policy of cultural assimilation, it stressed the value of African cultural traditions. African Personality was a concept that attributed unique qualities to African culture predisposing Africans toward socialism.

come to us from elsewhere. Our professors, engineers, and economists content themselves with simply adding color—because often the only things they've brought back from the European universities of which they are the products are their degrees and their velvety adjectives and superlatives!

It is both necessary and urgent that our trained personnel and scribes learn that there is no such thing as unbiased writing. In these stormy times we cannot leave our enemies of yesterday and today with an exclusive monopoly over thought, imagination, and creativity.

Before it's too late—because it's already late—these elites, these men of Africa and the Third World, must come back to who they are—that is, to their societies and to the misery we have inherited. They must understand that the battle for a system of thought at the service of the disinherited masses is not in vain. They must understand too that they can only become credible on an international level by being genuinely inventive, that is, by painting a faithful picture of their people. This picture must allow the people to achieve fundamental changes in the political and social situation, changes that allow us to break from the foreign domination and exploitation that leave our states no perspective other than bankruptcy.

This is what we glimpsed—we, the Burkinabè people—during the evening of August 4, 1983, when the first stars began to sparkle in the skies of our homeland. We had to take the leadership of the peasant revolts, signs of which were visible in a countryside that is panic-stricken by the advancing desert, exhausted by hunger and thirst, and abandoned. We had to give meaning to the brewing revolt of the idle urban masses, frustrated and weary of seeing limousines driving the elites around, elites that were out of touch, succeeding one another at the helm of state while offering the urban masses nothing but false solutions elaborated and conceived by the minds of others. We had to give an ideological soul to the just struggles of our popular masses as they mobilized against the monster of imperialism. The passing revolt, the simple brushfire, had to be replaced forever with the revolution, the permanent struggle against all forms of domination.

Others have explained before me, and others will explain after me, the extent to which the chasm has widened between the affluent peoples and those who aspire only to eat their fill, quench their thirst, survive, and preserve their dignity. But no one can imagine to what extent "the poor man's grain" in our countries "has fattened the rich man's cow"!

In the case of the former Upper Volta, the process was even more striking. We represented a wondrous condensation, the epitome of all the calamities that have ever befallen the so-called developing countries. The example of foreign aid, presented as a panacea and often heralded without rhyme or reason, bears eloquent witness to this fact. Very few countries have been inundated like mine with all kinds of aid. Theoretically, this aid is supposed to work in the interests of our development. In the case of what was formerly Upper Volta, one searches in vain for a sign of anything having to do with development. The men in power, either out of naiveté or class selfishness, could not or would not take control of this influx from abroad, understand its significance, or raise demands in the interests of our people.

In his book, *Le Sahel demain* [The Sahel of tomorrow], Jacques Giri, with a good deal of common sense, analyzes a table published in 1983 by the Sahel Club, and draws the conclusion that because of its nature and the mechanisms in place, aid to the Sahel helps only with bare survival.

Thirty percent of this aid, he stresses, serves simply to keep the Sahel alive. According to Jacques Giri, the only goal of this foreign aid is to continue developing nonproductive sectors, saddling our meager budgets with unbearably heavy expenditures, disorganizing our countryside, widening our balance of trade deficit, and accelerating our indebtedness.

Just a few images to describe the former Upper Volta: 7 million inhabitants, with over 6 million peasants; an infant mortality rate estimated at 180 per 1,000; an average life expectancy limited to 40 years; an illiteracy rate of up to 98 percent, if we define as literate anyone who can read, write, and speak a language; 1 doctor for 50,000 inhabitants; 16 percent of school-age youth attending school; and, finally, a per capita Gross Domestic Product of 53,356 CFA francs, or barely more than 100 U.S. dollars.

The diagnosis was clearly somber. The root of the disease was political. The treatment could only be political.

Of course, we encourage aid that aids us in doing away with aid. But in general, welfare and aid policies have only ended up disorganizing us, subjugating us, and robbing us of a sense of responsibility for our own economic, political, and cultural affairs.

We chose to risk new paths to achieve greater well-being. We chose to apply new techniques. We chose to look for forms of organization better suited to our civilization, flatly and definitively rejecting all forms of outside diktats, in order to lay the foundations for achieving a level of dignity equal to our ambitions. Refusing to accept a state of survival, easing the pressures, liberating our countryside from medieval stagnation or even regression, democratizing our society, opening minds to a world of collective responsibility in order to dare to invent the future. Shattering the administrative apparatus, then rebuilding it with a new kind of government employee, immersing our army in the people through productive labor and reminding it constantly that without patriotic political education, a soldier is only a potential criminal. Such is our political program.

On the level of economic management, we're learning to live modestly, to accept and impose austerity on ourselves in order to be able to carry out ambitious projects.

Thanks to the example of the National Solidarity Fund, which is financed by voluntary contributions, we're already beginning to find answers to the harsh questions posed by the drought. We have supported and applied the Alma Ata principles by widening the range of primary health-care services. We've adopted the GOBI FFF Strategy recommended by UNICEF as our own, making it government policy.[3]

Through the United Nations Sahel Office (UNSO), we believe the UN should enable the countries affected by the drought to set up a medium- and long-term plan to achieve food self-sufficiency.

To prepare for the twenty-first century, we have launched a huge campaign to educate and train our children in a new kind of school, financed by the creation of a special "Teach our children" raffle. Through the salutary action of the Committees for the Defense of the Revolution, we have launched a vast program to build public housing (500 units

---

3. The Alma Ata principles of the World Health Organization (WHO) and the United Nations International Children's Emergency Fund (UNICEF) emphasized proper nutrition, safe water, sanitation systems, maternal and child health care, immunization, and a reserve of basic medicine. UNICEF's GOBI FFF Strategy, focused on women and children, includes treating diarrhea-caused dehydration with an inexpensive solution of clean water, glucose, and salts; breastfeeding; immunization against six major communicable diseases; and education.

in three months), roads, small reservoirs, and so on. Our economic aspiration is to create a situation where every Burkinabè can at least use his brain and hands to invent and create enough to ensure him two meals a day and drinking water.

We swear, we proclaim, that from now on nothing in Burkina Faso will be done without the participation of the Burkinabè. Nothing that we have not first decided and worked out ourselves. There will be no further assaults on our sense of decency and our dignity.

Armed with this conviction, we would like our words to embrace all who suffer in the flesh and all whose dignity is flouted by a handful of men or by a system that is crushing them. To all of you listening to me, allow me to say: I speak not only on behalf of my beloved Burkina Faso, but also on behalf of all those who are in pain somewhere.

I speak on behalf of the millions of human beings who are in ghettos because they have black skin or because they come from different cultures, and who enjoy a status barely above that of an animal.

I suffer on behalf of the Indians who have been massacred, crushed, humiliated, and confined for centuries on reservations in order to prevent them from aspiring to any rights and to prevent them from enriching their culture through joyful union with other cultures, including the culture of the invader.

I cry out on behalf of those thrown out of work by a system that is structurally unjust and periodically unhinged, who are reduced to only glimpsing in life a reflection of the lives of the affluent.

I speak on behalf of women the world over, who suffer from a male-imposed system of exploitation. As far as we're concerned, we are ready to welcome suggestions from anywhere in the world that enable us to achieve the total fulfillment of Burkinabè women. In exchange, we offer to share with all countries the positive experience we have begun, with women now present at every level of the state apparatus and social life in Burkina Faso. Women who struggle and who proclaim with us that the slave who is not able to take charge of his own revolt deserves no pity for his lot. This slave alone will be responsible for his own misfortune if he harbors illusions in the dubious generosity of a master pretending to set him free. Freedom can be won only through struggle, and we call on all our sisters of all races to go on the offensive to conquer their rights.

I speak on behalf of the mothers of our destitute countries who watch their children die of malaria or diarrhea, unaware that simple means to save them exist. The science of the multinationals does not offer them these means, preferring to invest in cosmetics laboratories and plastic surgery to satisfy the whims of a few women or men whose smart appearance is threatened by too many calories in their overly rich meals, the regularity of which would make you—or rather us from the Sahel—dizzy. We have decided to adopt and popularize these simple means, recommended by the WHO and UNICEF.

I speak, too, on behalf of the child. The child of a poor man who is hungry and who furtively eyes the accumulation of abundance in a store for the rich. The store protected by a thick plate glass window. The window protected by impregnable shutters. The shutters guarded by a policeman with a helmet, gloves, and armed with a billy club. The policeman posted there by the father of another child, who will come and serve himself—or rather be served— because he offers guarantees of representing the capitalistic norms of the system, which he corresponds to.

I speak on behalf of artists—poets, painters, sculptors,

musicians, and actors—good men who see their art pros-
tituted by the alchemy of show-business tricks.

I cry out on behalf of journalists who are either reduced
to silence or to lies in order not to suffer the harsh law of
unemployment.

I protest on behalf of the athletes of the entire world
whose muscles are exploited by political systems or by
modern-day slave merchants.

My country is brimming with all the misfortunes of the
peoples of the world, a painful synthesis of all humanity's
suffering, but also—and above all—of the promise of our
struggles. This is why my heart beats naturally on behalf
of the sick who anxiously scan the horizons of a science
monopolized by arms merchants.

My thoughts go out to all those affected by the destruction of nature and to those 30 million who will die as they
do each year, struck down by the formidable weapon of
hunger. As a military man, I cannot forget the soldier who
is obeying orders, his finger on the trigger, who knows the
bullet being fired bears only the message of death.

Finally, it fills me with indignation to think of the Palestinians, who an inhuman humanity has decided to re-
place with another people—a people martyred only yesterday. I think of this valiant Palestinian people, that is,
these shattered families wandering across the world in
search of refuge. Courageous, determined, stoic, and un-
tiring, the Palestinians remind every human conscience
of the moral necessity and obligation to respect the rights
of a people. Along with their Jewish brothers, they are
anti-Zionists.

At the side of my brother soldiers of Iran and Iraq who
are dying in a fratricidal and suicidal war, I wish also to
feel close to my comrades of Nicaragua, whose harbors
are mined, whose villages are bombed, and who, despite

everything, face their destiny with courage and clear-headedness. I suffer with all those in Latin America who suffer from the stranglehold of imperialism.

I wish to stand on the side of the Afghan and Irish peoples, on the side of the peoples of Grenada and East Timor, each of whom is searching for happiness based on their dignity and the laws of their own culture.[4]

I protest here on behalf of all those who vainly seek a forum in this world where they can make their voice heard and have it genuinely taken into consideration. Many have preceded me at this podium and others will follow. But only a few will make the decisions. Yet we are officially presented as being equals. Well, I am acting as spokesperson for all those who vainly seek a forum in this world where they can make themselves heard. So yes, I wish to speak on behalf of all "those left behind," for "I am human, nothing that is human is alien to me."

Our revolution in Burkina Faso embraces the misfortunes of all peoples. It also draws inspiration from all of man's experiences since his first breath. We wish to be the heirs of all the world's revolutions and all the liberation struggles of the peoples of the Third World. Our eyes are on the profound upheavals that have transformed the world. We draw the lessons of the American Revolution, the lessons of its victory over colonial domination and the consequences of that victory. We adopt as our own the affirmation of the Doctrine whereby Europeans must

---

4. These were all countries under military occupation when this speech was given. Afghanistan had been occupied since 1979 by troops from the Soviet Union; northern Ireland remained a British colony brutally repressed by London; the Caribbean island of Grenada had been invaded by the U.S. army in October 1983; and the former Portuguese colony of East Timor in the Pacific had been invaded by Indonesia in 1975 and forcibly annexed.

not intervene in American affairs, nor Americans in European affairs. Just as Monroe proclaimed "America to the Americans" in 1823, we echo this today by saying "Africa to the Africans," "Burkina to the Burkinabè."

The French Revolution of 1789, which overturned the foundations of absolutism, taught us the connection between the rights of man and the rights of peoples to liberty. The great revolution of October 1917 [in Russia] transformed the world, brought victory to the proletariat, shook the foundations of capitalism, and made possible the Paris Commune's dreams of justice.[5]

Open to all the winds of the will of the peoples of the world and their revolutions, having also learned from some terrible failures that led to tragic violations of human rights, we wish to retain only the core of purity from each revolution. This prevents us from becoming subservient to the realities of others, even when we share common ground because of our ideas.

Mr. President:

It is no longer possible to keep up the deception. The new international economic order for which we fight and will continue to fight can be achieved only if we succeed in destroying the old order that has ignored us; if we impose our rightful place in the political organization of the world; and if, conscious of our importance in the world, we obtain the right to participate in discussions and decisions on the mechanisms governing trade, the economy, and currencies on a global scale.

The new international economic order should simply be inscribed alongside all the other rights of the people—the

---

5. In 1871 the insurgent workers and craftsmen of Paris established the first workers government in history, the Paris Commune. It was crushed in blood by the troops of the French bourgeoisie.

right to independence, to the free choice of governmental forms and structures—like the right to development. And like all the peoples' rights, it is conquered in struggle and by the struggle of the people. It will never be the result of an act of generosity from the powers that be.

I personally maintain unshakable confidence—a confidence shared by the immense community of Nonaligned countries—that, under the pounding blows of the howling anguish of our peoples, our group will maintain its cohesion, strengthen its collective bargaining power, find allies among all nations, and begin, together with those who can still hear us, to organize a genuinely new international system of economic relations.

Mr. President:

I agreed to come before this illustrious assembly to speak because, despite all the criticism made of it by some of its big contributors, the United Nations remains the ideal forum for our demands—the place where countries without voices must appear to be considered legitimate.

This is what our secretary general [Javier Pérez de Cuéllar] so correctly expressed when he wrote:

"The United Nations is unique in that it reflects the aspirations and frustrations of numerous countries and groupings around the world. One of its great merits is that all nations, including those that are weak, oppressed, and victims of injustice"—he's talking about us—"can, even when they are facing the harsh reality of power, come and find a tribune to be heard. Though a just cause may meet with misfortune or indifference, it can nevertheless find an echo in the United Nations. This characteristic of our organization has not always been appreciated, but it is nonetheless essential."

There can be no better definition of the meaning and

significance of our organization.

This is why it is a pressing need for each of us to con-solidate the foundations of our organization, to give it the means to act. We therefore approve the proposals made along these lines by the secretary general to extricate the organization from numerous dead ends, which have been carefully fostered by big-power maneuvering to discredit the UN in the eyes of public opinion.

Mr. President:

Recognizing the merits, however limited, of our organi-zation, I can only rejoice to see it welcome new members. This is why the Burkinabè delegation salutes the admis-sion of the 159th member of our organization: the state of Brunei Darussalam.

Due to the folly of those into whose hands the leader-ship of the world has fallen by quirk of fate, the Movement of Nonaligned Countries—of which I hope Brunei Darus-salam will soon become a member—is compelled to con-sider the fight for disarmament to be one of the permanent goals of its struggle. This is an essential aspect and a basic condition of our right to development.

In our opinion, we need serious studies that take into account all the elements that have led to the calamities that have befallen the world. In this regard, President Fi-del Castro expressed our point of view admirably in 1979 at the opening of the Sixth Summit Conference of Non-aligned Countries when he declared:

"Three hundred billion dollars is enough to build 600,000 schools a year with a capacity of 400 million children; or 60 million comfortable homes with a capacity of 300 million people; or 50,000 hospitals with 18 million beds; or 20,000 factories to provide employment for more than 20 million workers; or make possible the irrigation of 150 million hectares of land, which with an adequate technical level could provide food for a billion people."[6]

Multiplying these figures today by ten—and I'm sure this would fall short of reality—we realize what humanity squanders every year in the military field, that is, against peace.

One easily sees why the masses' indignation is rapidly transformed into revolt and revolution at the sight of the crumbs thrown their way in the degrading form of a little aid, sometimes tied to frankly despicable conditions. So it is clear why in the fight for development we refer to ourselves as tireless militants for peace.

We pledge to fight to ease tensions, to introduce principles of civilized life into international relations, and to extend them to all regions of the world. This means that we can no longer passively watch various concepts being bandied about. We reiterate our determination to be active proponents of peace; to take our place in the fight for disarmament; and finally to act as a decisive factor in international politics, completely unfettered by any of the major powers, whatever their plans may be.

But the quest for peace goes hand in hand with the firm application of the right of countries to independence, of peoples to liberty, and of nations to an autonomous existence. On this score the most pitiful and appalling—yes, the most appalling—record in terms of arrogance, insolence, and incredible stubbornness, is held by a small country in the Middle East, Israel. With the complicity of its powerful protector, the United States—which words cannot describe—Israel has continued to defy the international community for more than twenty years.

---

6. Fidel Castro's speech to the Nonaligned summit meeting on September 3, 1979, can be found in *Fidel Castro Speeches: Cuba's Internationalist Foreign Policy 1975-80* (New York: Pathfinder, 1981).

Scorning history, which only yesterday condemned each Jew to the horror of the gas chamber, Israel has now ended up inflicting on others an ordeal that was once its own. In any case, Israel, whose people we love for their courage and sacrifices of yesterday, must be made aware that conditions for its own tranquility cannot be achieved through military might financed from abroad. Israel must begin to learn how to become a nation like others and among others.

For the present, from up here at this rostrum, we want to assert our militant and active solidarity toward the combatants—women and men—of the wonderful people of Palestine, because we know that no suffering lasts forever.

Mr. President:

In analyzing the prevailing economic and political situation in Africa, we cannot fail to emphasize the deep concerns we harbor regarding the dangerous challenges made to the rights of peoples by certain nations which, secure in their alliances, openly scorn international moral standards.

Of course, we have the right to be delighted by the decision to withdraw foreign troops from Chad, so that without intermediaries Chadians can seek among themselves the means to end this fratricidal war and finally give their people, who have wept through so many winters, the means to dry their tears.[7]

Despite some progress registered here and there by the African peoples in their struggle for economic emancipation, however, our continent continues to reflect the basic

---

7. A former French colony in Central Africa, Chad was gripped by a recurrent civil war between factions supported by France in the south and Libya in the north. Paris intervened militarily in 1968-72, 1977-79, 1983-84, and 1986 to the present. Libyan troops occupied the north from 1983 to 1987.

reality of the conflicts between the major powers. We continue to bear the intolerable difficulties of the contemporary world.

This is why we hold the fate meted out to the people of Western Sahara by the Kingdom of Morocco to be unacceptable, and we unconditionally condemn it. Morocco is using delaying tactics to postpone a decision that, in any case, will be imposed on it by the will of the Saharawi people. Having personally visited the regions liberated by the Saharawi people, I am convinced that nothing will be able to impede any longer their march toward the total liberation of their country, under the militant and enlightened leadership of the Polisario Front.[8]

Mr. President:

I do not wish to dwell too much on the question of Mayotte and the islands of the Malagasy archipelago. When things are clear, when principles are obvious, there is no need to elaborate. Mayotte belongs to the Comoros. The islands of the archipelago belong to Madagascar.[9]

In Latin America, we salute the initiative by the Contadora Group, which marks a positive stage in the search for a just solution to the prevailing explosive situation. On

---

8. A former Spanish colony, Western Sahara was militarily occupied by Morocco and Mauritania in 1976 as Madrid pulled out. In face of a political struggle and guerrilla insurgency by the Polisario Front and the government in exile it formed, the Sahrawi Arab Democratic Republic, Mauritania withdrew in 1979, but the Moroccan government annexed the whole territory. The Saharawi people have continued to wage a struggle for independence ever since.

9. Three of the four islands making up the Comoros archipelago in the Indian Ocean near Mozambique gained independence from France in 1975. The fourth, Mayotte, remains a French colony.

The French-controlled islands off Madagascar include Europa, Bassas da India, Juan de Nova, the Iles Glorieuses, and Tromelin.

behalf of the revolutionary people of Nicaragua, Commander Daniel Ortega has made concrete proposals here and asked fundamental questions of the appropriate people. We expect to see peace take hold in his country and in Central America October 15 and thereafter, and we call on world public opinion to bear witness to what happens.[10]

Just as we condemned foreign aggression against the island of Grenada, we also denounce all foreign interventions. Therefore we cannot remain silent about foreign military intervention in Afghanistan.

There is, however, one particular question of such gravity that it demands a frank and decisive answer from each of us. As you might imagine, this question can be none other than that of South Africa. The incredible arrogance of that country toward all the nations of the world—even toward those who support the terrorism it has built into a system designed to physically liquidate the country's Black majority—and the contempt with which it treats all our resolutions, are among the weightiest concerns of today's world.

But the most tragic thing is not that South Africa has placed itself outside the international community because of the despicable character of its apartheid laws. Even less that it continues to illegally keep Namibia under the boot of colonialism and racism. Or that it behaves toward its neighbors with the impunity of a gangster. No, the most despicable, the most humiliating thing for the human conscience, is that it has managed to make "ordinary"

_____

10. Addressing the UN General Assembly on October 2, 1984, Daniel Ortega had warned that the U.S. government planned to escalate its attacks against Nicaragua to disrupt the November 4 presidential elections there. According to information obtained by the Nicaraguan government, the escalation was to begin around October 15.

the misfortune of millions of human beings who have nothing but their chests and the heroism of their bare hands with which to defend themselves. Secure in the complicity of the major powers, knowing that some will even actively intervene on its behalf, counting too on the criminal collaboration of a few wretched leaders of African countries, the white minority makes no bones about mocking the feelings of all peoples everywhere across the world, who consider intolerable the savagery of the methods employed.

There was a time when international brigades were formed to defend the honor of nations whose dignity had been assaulted. Today, despite the festering wounds we all bear, we are going to vote for resolutions whose only purpose, we will be told, is to bring to its senses this nation of pirates, which "destroys a smile like hail kills flowers."

Mr. President:

We will soon be celebrating the 150th anniversary of the emancipation of slaves by the British Empire. My delegation supports the proposal made by the countries of Antigua and Barbados to commemorate this event in a major way, an event whose meaning has taken on very great importance for the African countries and for the Black world. In our opinion, everything that is done, said, or organized around the world as part of the commemorative ceremonies should stress the terrible price paid by Africa and the Black world for the development of human civilization. A price paid without receiving anything in return, and which no doubt explains the reasons for the current tragedy on our continent.

It is our blood that fed the rapid development of capitalism, that made possible our current state of dependence, and that consolidated our underdevelopment. The truth can no longer be avoided, the numbers can no longer be doctored. For every Black person who made it to the plantations, at least five others suffered death or mutilation. I purposely leave aside the devastation of our continent and its consequences.

Mr. President:

If, thanks to you and with the help of the secretary general, the entire world can be convinced of that truth on the occasion of this anniversary, then it will understand why we desire peace between nations with every fiber of our being. And why we demand and lay claim to our right to development on the basis of total equality, through the organization and redistribution of human resources.

Of all the human races, we belong to those who have suffered most. That's why we Burkinabè have solemnly promised ourselves never again to accept the slightest denial of justice on the slightest bit of this earth. It is the memory of this suffering that places us at the side of the PLO against the armed bands of Israel. It is the memory of this suffering that leads us, on the one hand, to support the ANC and SWAPO, and makes it intolerable to us on the other that South Africa harbors men who torch the world in the name of being white. Finally, it is this same memory that leads us to place in the United Nations all our faith regarding shared duty, shared effort, and shared hope.

We call for intensifying throughout the world the campaign to free Nelson Mandela and guarantee his actual presence at the next session of the UN General Assembly. This will be a victory we can be proud of together. In memory of our sufferings and as a collective pardon, an International Prize for Human Reconciliation should be created, to be awarded to all those whose research has contributed to defending human rights. All the space research budgets should be cut by 1 percent, and the funds devoted to research in health and the restoration of the environment, which has been disturbed by all these fireworks harmful to the ecosystem.

We also propose that the structures of the UN be rethought and that we put a stop to that scandal known as the right of veto. It is true that the pernicious effects of its misuse have been mitigated by the vigilance of some of those who hold a veto. However, nothing justifies such a right—neither the size of the countries that hold it nor their wealth.

There are those who justify such iniquity by citing the price paid during the last world war. The nations that have granted themselves these rights should know that each of us, too, has an uncle or a father who, like thousands of other innocent people, was torn from the Third World to defend rights flouted by Hitler's hordes. Our flesh, too, bears the scars of Nazi bullets. So the arrogance of the big powers should cease—the powers that miss no opportunity to challenge the rights of the peoples of the world. Africa's absence from the club of those holding the right of veto is unjust and must cease.

Finally, my delegation would not be fulfilling all its duties if it failed to demand the suspension of Israel and the outright expulsion of South Africa from our organization. With the benefit of time, when these countries have carried out the transformation that returns them to the international community, each of us, starting with my country, should welcome them with kindness and guide their first steps.

We want to reaffirm our confidence in the United Nations. We are indebted to it for the work carried out by its agencies in Burkina Faso and for their presence at our side in the difficult times we are going through. We are grateful to the members of the Security Council for having allowed us to preside over the work of the council twice this year. We would simply hope to see the council adopt and apply the principle of fighting against the extermination of 30 million human beings every year by the hunger weapon, which today wreaks more devastation than the nuclear weapon.

This confidence and faith in the organization compels me to thank the secretary general, Mr. Javier Pérez de Cuéllar, for the much appreciated visit he made to us to see firsthand the harsh realities of our existence and obtain an accurate picture of the aridness of the Sahel, and the tragedy of the conquering desert.

I could not end without paying tribute to the eminent qualities of our president [Paul Lusaka of Zambia], who, with the perceptiveness for which we know him, will ably lead the work of this Thirty-ninth Session.

Mr. President:

I have traveled thousands of kilometers. I have come here to ask each of you to put our efforts together so that the arrogance of those who are wrong ceases, so that the sad spectacle of children dying of hunger vanishes, so that ignorance disappears, so that the legitimate revolt of the people triumphs, so that the sound of weapons falls silent, and so that finally, as we fight for the survival of humanity, united by a single will, we are able to sing together with the great poet Novalis:

"Soon the stars will revisit the earth they left during the age of obscurity. The sun will lay down its harsh specter and once again will become one star among many. All the races of the world will come together anew, after a long separation. Orphaned families of yore will be reunited and each day will be a day of reunification and renewed embraces. Then the inhabitants of olden times will return to the earth, in every tomb the extinguished cinders will be rekindled, and everywhere the flames of life will burn again. Old dwelling places will be rebuilt, the olden times will be born again, and history will be the dream of the present stretching to infinity."

Homeland or death, we will win!

Thank you.

Sankara outside Ouagadougou, August 1985.

MARLA PUZISS / MILITANT

UNITED NATIONS

Top: Sankara planting tree during mobilization to halt the spread of the desert, August 1985. **Bottom**: Women in Burkina Faso terrace soil to control erosion, April 1986.

Imperialism is the arsonist of our forests and savannas

My homeland, Burkina Faso, is without question one of the rare countries on this planet justified in calling itself and viewing itself as a distillation of all the natural evils from which mankind still suffers at the end of this twentieth century.

Eight million Burkinabè have painfully internalized this reality for twenty-three years. They have watched their mothers, fathers, daughters, and sons die, with hunger, famine, disease, and ignorance decimating them by the hundreds. With tears in their eyes, they have watched ponds and rivers dry up. Since 1973 they have seen the environment deteriorate, trees die, and the desert invade with giant strides. It is estimated that the desert in the Sahel advances at the rate of seven kilometers per year.

This speech was given at the first International Silva Conference for the Protection of the Trees and Forests in Paris. It was published in the February 14, 1986, issue of Carrefour africain.

Only by looking at these realities can one understand and accept the legitimate revolt that was born, that matured over a long period of time, and that finally erupted in an organized way the night of August 4, 1983, in the form of a democratic and popular revolution in Burkina Faso.

Here I am merely the humble spokesperson of a people who, having passively watched their natural environment die, refuse to watch themselves die. Since August 4, 1983, water, trees, and lives—if not survival itself—have been fundamental and sacred elements in all action taken by the National Council of the Revolution, which leads Burkina Faso.

In this regard, I am also compelled to pay tribute to the French people, to their government, and in particular to their president, Mr. François Mitterrand, for this initiative, which expresses the political genius and clear-sightedness of a people always open to the world and sensitive to its misery. Burkina Faso, situated in the heart of the Sahel, will always fully appreciate initiatives that are in perfect harmony with the most vital concerns of its people. The country will be present at them whenever it is necessary, in contrast to useless pleasure trips.

For nearly three years now, my people, the Burkinabè people, have been fighting a battle against the encroachment of the desert. So it was their duty to be here on this platform to talk about their experience, and also to benefit from the experience of other peoples from around the world. For nearly three years in Burkina Faso, every happy event—marriages, baptisms, award presentations, and visits by prominent individuals and others—is celebrated with a tree-planting ceremony.

To greet the new year 1986, all the schoolchildren and students of our capital, Ouagadougou, built more than 3,500 improved cookstoves with their own hands, offering them to their mothers. This was in addition to the 80,000 cookstoves made by the women themselves over the course of two years. This was their contribution to the national effort to reduce the consumption of firewood and to protect trees and life.

The ability to buy or simply rent one of the hundreds of the public dwellings built since August 4, 1983, is strictly conditional on the beneficiary promising to plant a minimum number of trees and to nurture them like the apple of his eye. Those who received these dwellings but were mindless of their commitment have already been evicted, thanks to the vigilance of our Committees for the Defense of the Revolution, committees that poisonous tongues take pleasure in systematically and unilaterally denigrating.

After having vaccinated throughout the national territory, in two weeks, 2.5 million children between the ages of nine months and fourteen years—children from Burkina Faso and from neighboring countries—against measles, meningitis, and yellow fever; after having sunk more than 150 wells assuring drinking water to the 20 or so districts in our capital that lacked this vital necessity until now; after having raised the literacy rate from 12 to 22 percent in two years—the Burkinabè people victoriously continue their struggle for a green Burkina.

Ten million trees were planted under the auspices of a fifteen-month People's Development Program, our first venture while awaiting the five-year plan. In the villages and in the developed river valleys, families must each plant one hundred trees per year.

The cutting and selling of firewood has been completely reorganized and is now strictly regulated. These measures range from the requirement to hold a lumber merchant's card, through respecting the zones designated for wood cutting, to the requirement to ensure reforestation of deforested areas. Today every Burkinabè town and village owns a wood grove, thus reviving an ancestral tradition.

Thanks to the effort to make the popular masses aware of their responsibilities, our urban centers are free of the plague of roaming livestock. In our countryside, our efforts focus on settling livestock in one place as a means of promoting intensive stockbreeding in order to fight against unrestrained nomadism.

All criminal acts of arson by those who burn the forest are subject to trial and sanctioning by the Popular Courts of Conciliation in the villages. The requirement of planting a certain number of trees is one of the sanctions issued by these courts.

From February 10 to March 20, more than 35,000 peasants—officials of the cooperative village groups—will take intensive, basic courses on the subjects of economic management and environmental organization and maintenance.

Since January 15 a vast operation called the "Popular Harvest of Forest Seeds" has been under way in Burkina for the purpose of supplying the 7,000 village nurseries. We sum up all of these activities under the label "the three battles."

Ladies and gentlemen:

My intention is not to heap unrestrained and inordinate praise on the modest revolutionary experience of my people with regard to the defense of the trees and forests. My intention is to speak as explicitly as possible about the profound changes occurring in the relationship between men and trees in Burkina Faso. My intention is to bear witness as accurately as possible to the birth and development of a deep and sincere love between Burkinabè men and trees in my homeland.

In doing this, we believe we are applying our theoretical conceptions on this, based on the specific ways and means of our Sahel reality, in the search for solutions to present and future dangers attacking trees all over the planet.

Our efforts and those of the entire community gathered here, your cumulative experience and ours, will surely guarantee us victory after victory in the struggle to save our trees, our environment, and, in short, our lives.

Excellencies, ladies and gentlemen:

I come to you in the hope that you are taking up a battle from which we cannot be absent, we who are attacked daily and who are waiting for the miracle of greenery to rise up from the courage to say what must be said. I have come to join with you in deploring the harshness of nature. But I have also come to denounce the ones whose selfishness is the source of his fellow man's misfortune. Colonial plunder has decimated our forests without the slightest thought of replenishing them for our tomorrows.

The unpunished disruption of the biosphere by savage and murderous forays on the land and in the air continues. One cannot say too much about the extent to which all these machines that spew fumes spread carnage. Those who have the technological means to find the culprits have no interest in doing so, and those who have an interest in doing so lack the technological means. They have only their intuition and their innermost conviction.

We are not against progress, but we do not want progress that is anarchic and criminally neglects the rights of others. We therefore wish to affirm that the battle against the encroachment of the desert is a battle to establish a balance between man, nature, and society. As such it is a political battle above all, and not an act of fate.

The creation of a Ministry of Water as a complement to the Ministry of the Environment and Tourism in my country demonstrates our desire to clearly formulate the problems in order to be able to resolve them. We must fight to find the financial means to exploit our existing water resources—drilling operations, reservoirs, and dams. This is the place to denounce the one-sided contracts and draconian conditions imposed by banks and other financial institutions that doom our projects in this field. It is these prohibitive conditions that lead to our countries' traumatizing debt and eliminate any meaningful maneuvering room.

Neither fallacious Malthusian arguments—and I assert that Africa remains an underpopulated continent—nor the vacation resorts pompously and demagogically christened "reforestation operations" provide an answer. We and our misery are spurned like bald and mangy dogs whose lamentations and cries disturb the peace and quiet of the manufacturers and merchants of misery.

That is why Burkina has proposed and continues to propose that at least 1 percent of the colossal sums of money sacrificed to the search for cohabitation with other stars and planets be used, by way of compensation, to finance projects to save trees and lives. We have not abandoned hope that a dialogue with the Martians might lead to the reconquest of Eden. But in the meantime, earthlings that we are, we also have the right to reject a choice limited simply to the alternatives of hell or purgatory.

Explained in this way, our struggle for the trees and forests is first and foremost a democratic and popular struggle. Because a handful of forestry engineers and experts getting themselves all worked up in a sterile and costly manner will never accomplish anything! Nor can the worked-up consciences of a multitude of forums and institutions—sincere and praiseworthy though they may be—make the Sahel green again, when we lack the funds to drill wells for drinking water a hundred meters deep, while money abounds to drill oil wells three thousand meters deep!

As Karl Marx said, those who live in a palace do not think about the same things, nor in the same way, as those who live in a hut. This struggle to defend the trees and forests is above all a struggle against imperialism. Because imperialism is the arsonist setting fire to our forests and our savannas.

Excellencies, ladies and gentlemen:

We rely on these revolutionary principles of struggle so that the green of abundance, joy, and happiness may take its rightful place. We believe in the power of the revolution to stop the death of our Faso and usher in a bright future for it.

Yes, the problem posed by the trees and forests is exclusively the problem of balance and harmony between the individual, society, and nature. This fight can be waged. We must not retreat in face of the immensity of the task. We must not turn away from the suffering of others, for the spread of the desert no longer knows any borders.

We can win this struggle if we choose to be architects and not simply bees.[1] It will be the victory of consciousness over instinct. The bee and the architect, yes! If the author of these lines will allow me, I will extend this twofold analogy to a threefold one: the bee, the architect, and the revolutionary architect.

Homeland or death, we will win!

Thank you.

---

1. Sankara is referring here to François Mitterrand's book, *L'abeille et l'architecte* (The bee and the architect).

Top: French colony of New Caledonia (Kanaky) in South Pacific, November 1984. Demonstrators wave Kanaky independence flag on barricade built during boycott of the colonial territorial assembly. **Bottom**: Demonstration of elderly people in a liberated zone of South Vietnam during early years of U.S. war against the country's struggle for national liberation in 1960s.

February 17, 1986

French enables us to communicate with other peoples in struggle

As a result of colonialism, we have become part of the French-speaking world, even though only 10 percent of Burkinabè speak the language. When we proclaim ourselves part of the French-speaking world, we do so with two preconditions: First, the French language is simply a means of expressing our reality. And second, like any language, French must open itself up to experiencing the sociological and historical realities of its own evolution.

Initially, for us, French was the language of the colonizer, the ultimate cultural and ideological vehicle of foreign and imperialist domination. But subsequently it was with this language that we were able to master the dialectical method of analyzing imperialism, putting us in a position

The First Francophone Summit was held in Paris February 17-19, 1986, attended by numerous heads of state of French-speaking countries. Burkina Faso was represented by Henri Zongo, minister of economic development. The following is the message to the conference that Sankara sent, which was published in Sidwaya.

to organize ourselves politically to fight and win.

Today in Burkina the Burkinabè people and their political leadership, the National Council of the Revolution, no longer use the French language as a vehicle of cultural alienation, but as a means of communication with other peoples.

Our presence at this conference is justified by the fact that from the point of view of the National Council of the Revolution, there are two French languages—the French spoken by those in metropolitan France, and the French spoken on the five continents.

In order to contribute to the enrichment of this universalized French, we intend to participate in this gathering and assess how the French language brings us closer to others. That's why I wish to thank the French authorities very sincerely for this welcome initiative.

It is through the intermediary of the French language that we, with our other African brothers, analyze our respective situations and seek to join efforts in common struggle.

It is through the intermediary of the French language that we shared the struggle of the Vietnamese people, and that we are reaching a better understanding of the cry of the Caledonian people.[1]

It is through the French language that we discover the richness of European culture, and defend the rights of our workers who have emigrated.

It is through the intermediary of the French language that we read the great educators of the proletariat and all those who, in a utopian or scientific manner, have put their

---

1. In the mid-1980s, the archipelago of New Caledonia, a French colony in the South Pacific, was the scene of widespread anticolonial mobilizations by the Kanaks, its native population.

pens at the service of the class struggle.

Finally, it is in French that we sing the *Internationale*, the hymn of the oppressed, of "the wretched of the earth."

We, for our part, interpret the universality of the French language to mean that we should use this language in conformity with our militant internationalism. We firmly believe in unity between the peoples. This unity will emerge from shared convictions, because we all suffer the same exploitation and the same oppression, no matter the social forms or how it may be dressed up over the course of time.

That is why, in our view, the French language, if it wishes to serve the ideals of 1789 more than those of the colonial expeditions, must accept other languages as expressions of the sensibilities of other peoples. In accepting other peoples, the French language must accept idioms and concepts that the realities of France have not permitted the French to get to know.

Who could, out of vanity or false pride, entangle themselves in circuitous formulations to convey in French, for example, the words *Islam* or *baraka*, when the Arabic language expresses these realities better than any other? Or the word *pianissimo*, the sweet musical expression from the other side of the Piedmont? Or the word *apartheid*—exported to France from Albion—without perfidiousness[2]—with all its Shakespearean richness.

To refuse to integrate the languages of others into French is to erect barriers of cultural chauvinism. Let us not forget that other languages have accepted terms from the French language that are untranslatable in their own. For example, English, with its "fair play," adopted from French the aristocratic and bourgeois term *champagne*. The Ger-

---

2. "Perfidious Albion," an epithet of French origin, refers to Britain.

man language, in its realpolitik, squarely admits, without beating around the bush, the French word *arrangement.* Finally, Peul, Mooré, Bantu, Wolof, and many other African languages have assimilated, with suppressed anger, the oppressive and exploitative terms *impôts* [taxes], *corvée,* and *prison.*

This diversity [*diversité*] brings us together in the French-speaking family. We make it rhyme with friendship [*amitié*] and fraternity [*fraternité*].

To refuse to integrate other languages is to be unaware of the roots and history of one's own. Every language is the product of several others, today more so than in the past, because of the cultural permeability created in these modern times by the powerful means of communication. To reject other languages is to adopt a rigid attitude against progress, and that approach stems from an ideology inspired by reaction.

Burkina Faso opens itself to other peoples and counts heavily on the culture of others to grow richer. For we are convinced that we are headed toward a universal civilization that will lead us to a universal language. This is the framework for our use of French.

For the genuine progress of humanity! Forward!

Homeland or death, we will win!

Top: Literacy campaign, Kamboince, March 1986. **Bottom**: Construction of Cité An III housing complex on General Sandino Street, Ouagadougou, 1987. The street was named after the leader of the liberation war in Nicaragua against the U.S. military occupation in the 1920s and '30s.

Top: Che Guevara and Cuban internationalist volunteers in Congo, 1965, to assist Congolese forces fighting proimperialist regime. **Bottom**: Demonstrators in South Africa denounce the racist system of apartheid and demand the government unban the African National Congress, mid-1980s.

You cannot kill ideas

A tribute to Che Guevara

We've come this morning, in a modest way, to open this exhibition that seeks to trace the life and work of Che. At the same time, we want to tell the whole world today that for us Che Guevara is not dead. Because throughout the world there are centers of struggle where people strive for more freedom, more dignity, more justice, and more happiness. Throughout the world, people are fighting against oppression and domination; against colonialism, neocolonialism, and imperialism; and against class exploitation.

Dear friends, we join our voices with everyone in the world who remembers that one day a man called Che Gue-

A week before the overthrow of the revolutionary government and Sankara's assassination, he gave this speech in Ouagadougou at the inauguration of an exhibition honoring the life of Cuban revolutionary leader Ernesto Che Guevara, who had been killed exactly twenty years earlier. A Cuban delegation that included Guevara's son, Camilo Guevara March, was in attendance. Inaudible passages in the tape-recording of the speech are indicated by ellipses.

vara . . . his heart filled with faith, took up the struggle
alongside other men and, in so doing, succeeded in creating a spark that powerfully disturbed the forces of occupation in the world.

We simply want to say that a new era in Burkina Faso
has come, a new reality is on the march in our country.
That's how Che Guevara's call to action must be understood—Che, who wanted to light fires of struggle throughout the world.

Che Guevara was cut down by bullets, imperialist bullets, under Bolivian skies. And we say that for us, Che
Guevara is not dead.

One of the beautiful phrases often recalled by revolutionaries, by the great Cuban revolutionaries, is the one
that Che's friend, his companion in struggle, his comrade,
his brother, Fidel Castro himself repeated. He heard it
from the mouth of a man of the people one day during the
struggle—one of Batista's officers who, despite being part
of that reactionary, repressive army, managed to connect
with the forces fighting for the well-being of the Cuban
people. Right after the assault on the Moncada garrison
had failed, when those who had attempted it were about
to be put to death by the guns of Batista's army—they were
going to be shot—the officer said simply, "Don't shoot, you
cannot kill ideas."[1]

It's true, you cannot kill ideas. Ideas do not die. That's

1. On July 26, 1953, some 160 combatants led by Fidel Castro attacked the
Moncada garrison in Santiago de Cuba, and the garrison in the nearby
town of Bayamo, with the goal of initiating a popular uprising against
the U.S.-backed dictatorship of Fulgencio Batista. After the attack, Batista's forces massacred more than fifty of the captured revolutionaries.
Despite its failure, the Moncada attack marked the opening volley of the
revolutionary struggle that culminated less than six years later in the
overthrow of the dictatorship in January 1959.

why Che Guevara, an embodiment of revolutionary ideas and self-sacrifice, is not dead. You have come here today [from Cuba], and we draw inspiration from you.

Che Guevara, an Argentine according to his passport, became an adopted Cuban through the blood and sweat he shed for the Cuban people. He became, above all, a citizen of the free world—the free world that we're building together. That's why we say that Che Guevara is also African and Burkinabè.

Che Guevara called his beret *la boina*. He made that beret and its star known almost everywhere in Africa. From the north to the south, Africa remembers Che Guevara.

Bold young people—young people thirsting for dignity, thirsting for courage, thirsting also for ideas and for the vitality he symbolized in Africa—sought out Che Guevara in order to drink from the source, the invigorating source represented in the world by this revolutionary captain. Some of the few who had the opportunity and honor of being in Che's presence, and who are still alive, are here among us today.

Che is Burkinabè. He is Burkinabè because he participates in our struggle. He is Burkinabè because his ideas inspire us and are inscribed in our Political Orientation Speech. He is Burkinabè because his star is stamped on our banner. He is Burkinabè because some of his ideas live in each of us in the daily struggle we wage.

Che is a man, but a man who knew how to show us and teach us that we can dare to have confidence in ourselves and our abilities. Che is among us.

What is Che, I'd like to ask? Che, to us, is above all conviction, revolutionary conviction, revolutionary faith in what you're doing, the conviction that victory belongs to us, and that struggle is our only recourse.

Che is also a sense of humanity. Humanity—this expression of generosity and self-sacrifice that made Che not only an Argentine, Cuban, and internationalist combatant, but also a man, with all the warmth of a man.

Che is also, and above all, demanding. The demanding character of one who had the good fortune to be born into a well-to-do family . . . Yet he was able to say no to those temptations, to turn his back on the easy road in order, on the contrary, to assert himself as a man of the people, a man who makes common cause with the people, a man who makes common cause with the suffering of others. Che's demanding character is what should inspire us the most.

Conviction, humanity, a demanding character—all this makes him Che. Those who are capable of mustering these virtues within themselves, those who are capable of mustering these qualities within themselves—this conviction, this humanity, and this demanding character—they can say that they are like Che—men among men, but, above all, revolutionaries among revolutionaries.

We have just looked at these pictures that trace part of Che's life as best they can. Despite their forceful expression, these images remain silent on the most crucial part of the man, the very part against which imperialism took aim. The bullets were aimed much more at Che's spirit than at his image. His picture is found the world over. His photo is in everyone's mind, and his silhouette is one of the best-known. So let's see to it that we're able to get to know Che better.

Let's draw closer to Che. Let's draw closer to him, not as we would a god, not as we would an idea—an image placed above men—but rather with the feeling that we're moving toward a brother who speaks to us and to whom we can also speak. We must see to it that revolutionaries draw inspiration from Che's spirit, that they too become internationalists, that they too, together with other men, learn how to build faith—faith in the struggle for change, in the struggle against imperialism and against capitalism.

As to you, Comrade Camilo Guevara, we certainly cannot speak of you as an orphaned son. Che belongs to all of us. He belongs to us as a heritage belonging to all revolutionaries. So you cannot feel alone and abandoned, finding as you do in each of us—we hope—brothers, sisters, friends, and comrades. Together with us today you are a citizen of Burkina, because you have followed resolutely in Che's footsteps—the Che who belongs to all of us, a father to us all.

Finally, let us remember Che simply as an embodiment of eternal romanticism, of fresh and invigorating youth, and at the same time of the clear-sightedness, wisdom, and devotion that only profound men, men with heart, can possess. Che was the seventeen-year-old youth. But Che was also the wisdom of a man of seventy-seven. This judicious combination is something we should achieve all the time. Che was both the heart that spoke, and the bold and vigorous hand that took action.

Comrades, I would like to thank our Cuban friends for the efforts they made to be with us. I would like to thank all those who traveled thousands of kilometers and crossed oceans to come here to Burkina Faso to remember Che.

I would also like to thank everyone whose personal contributions will ensure that this day will not be a mere date on the calendar, but will, above all, become days, many days in the year, many days over the years and centuries, making Che's spirit live eternally.

Comrades, I would finally like to express my joy that we have been able to immortalize Che's ideas here in Ouagadougou by naming this street after Che Guevara.

Every time we think of Che, let's try to be like him, and make this man, the combatant, live again. And especially, every time we think of acting in his spirit of self-sacrifice, by rejecting material goods that seek to alienate us, by refusing to take the easy road, by turning instead to education and the rigorous discipline of revolutionary morality—every time we try to act in this way, we will better serve Che's ideas, we will spread them more effectively.

Homeland or death, we will win!

INDEX

Afghanistan, 14, 70, 77
Africa, 14–15, 78, 80, 90; French imperialism and, 6, 31–32, 36, 75, 94; influence of Sankara in, 14–15, 23
African National Congress (ANC), 79
African Personality, 62
Agramonte, Manuel, 9
Agrarian reform, 11, 21, 51. *See also* Peasants
Agriculture, 51
Aid, foreign, 36, 64–65
Algeria, 31
Alma Ata principles, 66
American Revolution (1775–83), 12, 70
Angola, 17
Antigua, 78
Army: and Burkina revolution, 46–48, 66; under capitalism, 32, 45, 47, 48

Barbados, 78
Batista, Fulgencio, 100
Bishop, Maurice, 13
Blacks, 22, 67, 77, 78–79
Bobo-Dioulasso, 35
Bourgeoisie: and counterrevolution, 38, 45; groupings within, 33, 38–39, 43; political power of, 33, 39; speculating activities of, 39, 51; ties to imperialism, 39, 45
Brunei Darussalam, 73
Bureaucracy, 52
Burkinabè Revolution, 6–7, 23, 46; anti-imperialist character of, 43,

56, 60, 64, 69–70; August 1983 uprising, 29, 30–31, 37–38, 63–64; building new state machinery, 43, 44–45, 51, 65–66; class character of, 11, 21–22, 40–45; as heir to world's revolutions, 12, 71; part of world revolutionary movement, 17, 22–23, 55–56
Burkina Faso: class structure of, 33–34, 38–42; ethnic and national divisions in, 54–55; social conditions in, 6, 10, 21, 34–35, 37, 59, 65. *See also* Upper Volta

Capitalism, 34, 39, 41, 43, 78; as cause of social evils, 10, 24; revolutionary struggle against, 12, 71, 99. *See also* Bourgeoisie; Imperialism
Castro, Fidel, 10, 11, 73–74, 100
CFA franc, 36
Chad, 75
Civil servants, 37, 52
Class struggle, 61, 94–95
Committees for the Defense of the Revolution (CDRs), 66, 87; role in revolution, 44, 45, 48, 55
Communist International, 13
Communist Manifesto (Marx and Engels), 9–10
Comoros Islands, 76
Compaoré, Blaise, 7, 23
Contadora, 76
Cookstoves, 86–87
Counterrevolution, 42, 44; struggle

The Cuban Five

The Cuban Five
Who They Are
Why They Were Framed
Why They Should Be Free

Presents the facts on the worldwide struggle to free Gerardo Hernández, Ramón Labañino, Antonio Guerrero, Fernando González, and René González. Shows how this battle to defend the Five is part of the class struggle in the US, where millions of working people know how the courts and prisons are used to punish those who refuse to accept the conditions imposed on us by capitalism. $5. Also in Spanish and French.

Cuba and Angola
Fighting for Africa's Freedom and Our Own
1975–91

The story of Cuba's nearly 16-year internationalist mission to aid the people of Angola, in the words of those who made that history, including Fidel Castro, Nelson Mandela, and Raúl Castro. With a special feature by Gabriel García Márquez. Also includes accounts by three of the Cuban Five who fought in Angola. $12. Also in Spanish.

> "One of the ways our revolution will be judged in years to come is by how well we have solved the problems facing women."

FIDEL CASTRO, 1974

Women in Cuba: The Making of a Revolution Within the Revolution

Vilma Espín
Asela de los Santos
Yolanda Ferrer
$20

Women and Revolution: The Living Example of the Cuban Revolution

Asela de los Santos
Mary-Alice Waters
$7

As working people in Cuba fought to bring down a bloody tyranny in the 1950s, the unprecedented integration of women in the ranks and leadership of the struggle was not an aberration. It was intertwined with the proletarian course of the leadership of the Cuban Revolution from the start.

Women in Cuba: The Making of a Revolution Within the Revolution is the story of that revolution and how it transformed the women and men who made it. The book was introduced at the 2012 Havana International Book Fair by a panel of speakers from Cuba and the US.

Women and Revolution: The Living Example of the Cuban Revolution contains the presentations from that event.

Both titles also in Spanish.

New from Pathfinder!

Voices from Prison
The Cuban Five

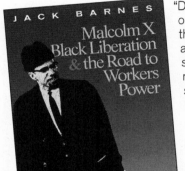

EXPAND YOUR REVOLUTIONARY LIBRARY

The Working Class and the Transformation of Learning
The Fraud of Education Reform under Capitalism
JACK BARNES

"Until society is reorganized so that education is a human activity from the time we are very young until the time we die, there will be no education worthy of working, creating humanity." $3. Also in Spanish, French, Swedish, Icelandic, Farsi, and Greek.

Thomas Sankara Speaks
The Burkina Faso Revolution, 1983–87
THOMAS SANKARA

Colonialism and imperialist domination have left a legacy of hunger, illiteracy, and economic backwardness in Africa. In 1983 the peasants and workers of Burkina Faso established a popular revolutionary government and began to combat the causes of such devastation. Thomas Sankara, who led that struggle, explains the example set for Africa and the world. $24. Also in French.

Cosmetics, Fashions, and the Exploitation of Women
JOSEPH HANSEN, EVELYN REED, MARY-ALICE WATERS

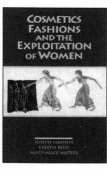

Sixty years ago, an article published in the socialist weekly the *Militant* sparked a lively debate on how the cosmetics and "fashion" industries play on the economic and emotional insecurities of women and youth to rake in profits. Today that exchange, contained in this book, a Marxist classic, offers an introduction to the origin of women's oppression and the struggle for liberation. $15. Also in Spanish.

WWW.PATHFINDERPRESS.COM

Cuba & Africa

HOW FAR WE SLAVES HAVE COME!
South Africa and Cuba in Today's World
NELSON MANDELA, FIDEL CASTRO
Speaking together in Cuba in 1991, Mandela
and Castro discuss the place in the history
of Africa of Cuba and Angola's victory over
the invading US-backed South African army,
and the resulting acceleration of the fight to
bring down the racist apartheid system. $10.
Also in Spanish.

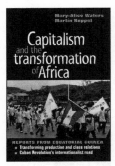

CAPITALISM AND
THE TRANSFORMATION OF AFRICA
Reports from Equatorial Guinea
MARY-ALICE WATERS, MARTÍN KOPPEL
An account of the transformation of production and
class relations in this Central African country, as it is
drawn deeper into the world market and both a capitalist
class and modern proletariat are born. Here also the
example of Cuba's socialist revolution comes alive in
the collaboration of Cuban volunteer medical brigades
helping to transform social conditions. Woven together, the outlines of a future to
be fought for today can be seen—a future in which the toilers of Africa have more
weight in world politics than ever before. $10. Also in Spanish.

CUBA'S INTERNATIONALIST FOREIGN POLICY
FIDEL CASTRO
Cuba's foreign policy, says Castro, starts "with the
subordination of Cuban positions to the international
needs of the struggle for socialism and national
liberation." Speeches from 1975–80 on solidarity with
Angola, Vietnam, the Nicaragua and Grenada revolutions,
and more. $23

www.pathfinderpress.com

New International

A MAGAZINE OF MARXIST POLITICS AND THEORY

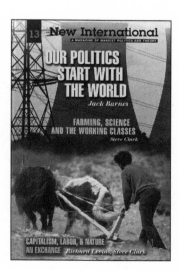

PATHFINDER AROUND THE WORLD

Visit our website for a complete list of titles and to place orders

www.pathfinderpress.com

PATHFINDER DISTRIBUTORS

UNITED STATES
(and Caribbean, Latin America, and East Asia)
> Pathfinder Books, 306 W. 37th St., 13th Floor
> New York, NY 10018

CANADA
> Pathfinder Books, 7107 St. Denis, Suite 204
> Montreal, QC H2S 2S5

UNITED KINGDOM
(and Europe, Africa, Middle East, and South Asia)
> Pathfinder Books, First Floor, 120 Bethnal Green Road
> (entrance in Brick Lane), London E2 6DG

AUSTRALIA
(and Southeast Asia and the Pacific)
> Pathfinder, Level 1, 3/281–287 Beamish St., Campsie, NSW 2194
> Postal address: P.O. Box 164, Campsie, NSW 2194

NEW ZEALAND
> Pathfinder, 188a Onehunga Mall, Onehunga, Auckland 1061
> Postal address: P.O. Box 3025, Auckland 1140